W9-BWY-392

ORCHESTRAL ACCENTS

RICHARD KORN

ORCHESTRAL

ACCENTS

BRIAR CLIFF COLLEGE
LIBRARY
SIOUX CITY, IOWA

FARRAR, STRAUS AND CUDAHY

NEW YORK

© 1956 by Richard Korn
Library of Congress catalog card number 56-5674
First printing, 1956
Manufactured in the United States of America by H. Wolff, New York
Design: Klaus M. Gemming

MT
75
.K8

to
P E G
who kept the light burning

45250

CONTENTS

ORCHESTRAL ACCENTS

INTRODUCTORY

Musical notation is at best an inadequate system; the marks written by composers on their score paper, if realized in sound strictly literally, will never serve to convey their creators' conceptions. Performers must breathe the life of their own creative capacities into the inanimate marks on the page. Among such marks are accents; and accent marks are as essential to proper musical performance as note marks, and similarly, are capable of interpretation in many different ways, according to the context.

This book will treat only of accents written in the score. Those which are not so written, being left to optional insertion by the performer, are outside its scope. All composers worthy of the name have judiciously sprinkled their scores with accents, on the sound principle that an aesthetic balance must be attained between performances devoid of accents and therefore pallid, and those so full of accents that the hearer's attention becomes saturated with constant overemphasis.

Accent marks occur in several forms—the symbol ∨, the symbol ∧, the symbol >, the symbol *sf* and its variants, and so on. The first two of these are special and relatively rare cases, and will be discussed in the Appendix; all the others, with certain exceptions to be noted, will be considered as, and shown to be, entirely mutually equivalent and interchangeable. Aside from such exceptions, and a few others to be mentioned, research in established musical literature has failed to disclose any instance where the *symbol* chosen to indicate the accent affects the *quality* of the accent to be applied. Most composers have their preferences for one or more of the symbols over the others; but the kind of emphasis thus indicated is determined *not by the symbol chosen* but *solely by the musical context.*

Obviously no survey of this size could exhaustively cover the subject. However, it is hoped that from it performers will be guided in their task by reference to this analysis of accents in representative examples of orchestral composition, selected in chronological order.

The present recorded state of understanding concerning accents is a confused, or at best a loose, one. For example, the definition of "sforzando" in *Grove's Dictionary* is as follows: "Sforzando (Sforzato), 'forced'; a direction usually found in its abbreviated forms *sf* or *sfz* referring to single notes or groups of notes which are to be especially emphasized. It is nearly equivalent to the accent >, but is less apt to be overlooked in performance, and is therefore used in all important passages." According to this definition, there is a difference between the two symbols, and it is due to the composer's idea of the slovenliness of his performers and to just how much the composer cared about each of his directions being noticed and carried out. The absurdity of this definition is further shown by its total lack of reference to the number of different kinds of emphasis available. Another useless definition is that of "rinforzando" in the same publication: " 'Reinforcing' or increasing in power. This word, or its abbreviations, *rinf.* or *rfz.*, is used to denote a sudden and brief *crescendo*. It is applied generally to a whole phrase, however short, and has the same meaning as *sforzando,* which is only applied to single notes. It is sometimes used in concerted music to give a momentary prominence to a subordinate part, as for instance in the Beethoven quartet, Op. 95, in the Allegretto, where the violoncello part is marked *rinforzando* when it has the second section of the principal subject of the movement." Further examples, these from Schirmer's *Pocket Manual of Musical Terms:* "Sforzando, sforzato (written *sfz, sf,* >, ∧, ⁓). A direction to perform the tone or chord with special stress, or marked and sudden emphasis." And again, "Rinforzando, rinforzato—with special emphasis; it indicates a sudden increase in loudness either for a tone or chord, or throughout a phrase or short passage." Finally, the definition of "accent" in *Grove's Dictionary* pertains only to unwritten, or "agogic" accents.

It is thus apparent that those who depend on the written word for their understanding of accents labor under a great handicap. For, as will be shown in these pages, accents are gently expressive, as well as forceful. Many practicing musicians are keenly aware of the diversity of accents, and how to apply each kind in its proper place. The writer is proud to acknowledge his indebtedness to many of them, and wishes to make it clear that he himself does not pretend to have formulated the principles expounded herein. On the contrary, he has occasionally been delighted to encounter in others an appreciation of them, as for instance this, from an article on "Conductors and Conducting" by Rupert Hughes: * "Take the first few measures of the Vorspiel to *Tristan und Isolde* for a familiar example; beginning with a single voice, there is a *crescendo* ending in a *sforzando,* which is generally taken as an abrupt and harsh shock. But *sf* is a term always relative to the context, and this particular example is surely meant to be a soft shudder of mingled love and anguish; so Anton Seidl took it and so does Richter." And there have been numerous concerts and recordings —notably Toscanini's of the overture to *L'Italiana in Algieri*—in which the performance of the accents has been exemplary.

Notwithstanding such rare and welcome preservations of flashes of insight, the present writer believes that there is still a useful service to perform in codifying a consistent and rational system of accentuation; and he humbly hopes that he will perform it satisfactorily.

* In *Famous Composers and Their Works,* New Series, edited by Philip Hale, published by J. B. Millet Co., Boston, 1900.

For the purposes of this survey, then, an accent is thus defined: some prominence, force, emphasis, stress, quality or intensity, imparted to a designated note, greater than that of its unaccented neighbors, and greater than what it would have if unaccented, which is an organic and integral part of the musical context, and the type of which is thus determined by that context. It can affect the performance of that note with respect to volume, tone quality, duration, or manner of attack, or any combination of these factors.

The various possible combinations of these factors making up the basic types of accent are tabulated as follows:

A. At starting point of tone only.
    1. Acute, simple.
    2. Acute, volume.
    3. Acute, color.
    4. Acute, both volume and color.
    5. Plain, volume.
    6. Plain, color.
    7. Plain, both volume and color.

B. At starting point of tone and thereafter.
    8. Acute, simple, lengthening.
    9. Acute, simple, shortening.
    10. Acute, volume.
    11. Acute, volume, lengthening.
    12. Acute, volume, shortening.
    13. Acute, color.
    14. Acute, color, lengthening.
    15. Acute, color, shortening.
    16. Acute, both volume and color.
    17. Acute, both volume and color, lengthening.
    18. Acute, both volume and color, shortening.
    19. Plain, volume.
    20. Plain, volume, lengthening.
    21. Plain, volume, shortening.
    22. Plain, color.
    23. Plain, color, lengthening.
    24. Plain, color, shortening.
    25. Plain, both volume and color.
    26. Plain, both volume and color, lengthening.
    27. Plain, both volume and color, shortening.

C. After starting point of tone only.
    28. Simple, lengthening.
    29. Simple, shortening.
    30. Volume.
    31. Volume, lengthening.
    32. Volume, shortening.
    33. Color.
    34. Color, lengthening.
    35. Color, shortening.
    36. Both volume and color.
    37. Both volume and color, lengthening.
    38. Both volume and color, shortening.

Compound types:
D. Combinations of classes A and C.
E. Other combinations (see explanation below).

The preceding table is thus explained. Class A pertains only to the initial instant of a sustained tone, or the whole of a *staccato* tone. "Acute" denotes the effect of an instantaneous "bite" at the inception of the tone. On the stringed instruments this is attained with a small quick jerk of the bow—sometimes with the whole arm, sometimes with the wrist alone, sometimes with both as the circumstances dictate; or if *pizzicato,* with a keener plucking than ordinarily. On the wind instruments, it is done with a hard tongue-stroke, as if pronouncing the letter T, instead of D as the player would simulate if there were no accent. In all respects other than that of this initial "bite" or "edge" the tone remains exactly as if unaccented; and the "bite" or "edge" is of a degree barely sufficient to distinguish the tone from an unaccented one. The foregoing applies equally to tones in all amounts of volume; it includes the tiny "edge" imparted to the almost inaudible tone, which accomplishes no more than to make a keen listener certain as to the point of the tone's inception, as well as the thrust that pierces a deafening tumult—and all gradations in between. A "plain" accent is one that does not have this initial "edge."

It should be here emphatically pointed out that in the above table accents have NOT been classified on the basis of relative dynamics—*i.e.,* in regard to degree of loudness. The reason, though, is solely the following, which must be borne clearly in mind throughout this survey: ACCENTS VARY WITH THE DYNAMICS ONLY IN VOLUME, NOT IN TYPE. In other words, the above table applies in its entirety to each and every degree of dynamics, in the manner of a sliding scale; for every shade of volume, the table can be repeatedly set forth fully as it stands. The AMOUNT OF FORCE—loudness or intensity—imparted to any of the 38 types of accent is determined by, and varies directly with, the AMOUNT OF FORCE prevalent in the surrounding musical texture, and with this only. Unless a contrast is clearly indicated (ordinarily by an accent of the types discussed in the appendix), ONLY such additional force, in whichever type of accent is called for, should be imparted as is necessary to audibly effectuate the accent TO THE MINIMUM EXTENT, with regard to the acoustic conditions of the given performance.

There is, however, one respect, and only one, in which the surrounding dynamics may affect the TYPE of accent: where the dynamics, CONSIDERED TOGETHER WITH ALL THE OTHER MUSICAL VALUES PRESENT, determine the CHARACTER OF THE MUSIC or the MUSICAL CONTEXT. For again, it is the latter alone which determines the TYPE of accent to be applied in each instance.

In the table the word "volume" is used to indicate the factor of a louder tone. In the types of accent in which the word appears, the tone is to be played with the minimum appreciable degree of loudness above that of an unaccented note, or a type lacking the factor of volume. There is no type of accent by which the accented tone is to be played *less* loudly than it would be without the accent. However, it may sometimes be found advisable, in order to effectuate an accent, to play surrounding *unaccented* notes with less force than if there were no accent present.

"Color," as encountered first in type 3, is a word with one general meaning which, however, allows of many infinitesimal variations: the enriched tone quality, produced in emphasizing the characteristic timbre of any given instrument, or in projecting more than ordinary vitality, warmth, intensity, weight, breadth, or "expression," or both, but in every case without increasing the dynamic strength. As there are hardly any two players of any instrument who produce these effects in exactly the same way or with identical results, it would serve little useful purpose to further particularize this point. Moreover, as is obvious, the "color" to be applied varies widely according to the context. Therefore, with no further elucidation here, let it suffice to be said that the performer should produce the indicated musical effect in terms of his own mechanism, background, style, personality, and feeling.

"Simple" in the table denotes the absence of the factors of both volume and color. In other words, the sustained portion of a tone with a "simple" accent is played exactly as if the tone were unaccented (unless there is a duration factor); and the only feature of an accent on a *staccato* tone thus accented is the "bite." (There can be no such thing as a plain simple accent; that could not possibly be any accent of any kind at all.) While one might suppose that simple accents are the preponderantly usual kind, further examination will show that such a supposition would be far from the truth; in fact, that kind is one of the most unusual.

In class B the effectuation of the accent is continued beyond the instant of the tone's inception; and ordinarily it will extend to the very termination of the tone. In this class a new factor appears, which concerns the duration of the tone. The terms "lengthening" and "shortening" denote, respectively, a prolongation of the accented tone beyond the duration it would normally have if unaccented—that is, a small amount less than its full mathematical duration (though the accent can never give any tone *more* than its complete value)—and a curtailment to something less than its normal duration. The duration factor, though it never occurs without one or more of the others, adds to expressive richness in many ways. One of them which can be pointed out here, is that prolongation itself adds intensity purely by making the hearer aware that conscious and concentrated human attention is being applied in the process of shaping the tone. Of course, in a legato melodic voice, this duration-modifying effect of an accent is inoperative, since each tone must be sustained to the utmost limit of its value anyway; but where the tones constituting a melodic voice are not slurred together, it can very well be operative, since the relative duration of the tones and any silent intervals between them is not ordinarily notated with precision and must be determined by all the interpretive resources that can be brought to bear.

The table does not make it clear whether the "bite" called for in types which include a volume factor must be stronger than in those which do not. But a moment's thought will show that in those which include the volume factor, it must be correspondingly stronger, as if the surrounding dynamics were on the same level as the accented note.

Class C, in which no part of the effect of the accent occurs at the inception of the tone, all of the accent's effect being imparted after the tone has already begun to sound, is the least frequent class. This is an effect which has not been largely utilized in the present body of musical literature, but which may well figure more prominently in music yet to be written.

The above covers the basic types of accent. In addition, there are two classes of compound types, which are not tabulated in detail because of their great complexity. Class D is that in which a class C accent is preceded (on the same note, of course) by a class A one, the combination not being a unified nuance (if it were, it would be in class B). Class E includes complex nuances consisting of different possible successions of the factors in classes B and/or C. Because the possible number of such combinations is so vast, the complete enumeration of them would be a cerebral exercise unnecessarily detailed for practical purposes, and therefore will not be made here. Instances of such accents will be noted as they are encountered.

The historical order chosen for this survey has been considered preferable to an analytic treatment, in which a given type of accent would be illustrated by examples from different periods and styles in juxtaposition. The meaning of each example will be understood more easily and fully in the setting of its own period and style.

The object of this survey, then, will be to demonstrate the relation between musical character and the interpretation of accents.

TWO

THE ORIGINS

Written accents first appear in orchestral music during the eighteenth century, in the composers younger than Bach and Handel. Those two masters left their scores so sparsely marked that their music furnishes no material for consideration in this survey. They would be dumfounded to discover that musicians of later days would consider their scores bare, since they wrote into them everything that musicians of their time could possibly need in the way of directions for performance. The directions which they left unwritten were matters of general understanding and well-established convention, which constitute a large field of knowledge in itself, and on which many years of scholarly research can profitably be spent. It is outrageous how often the works of those masters are played and recorded—one cannot truly say performed—without even the introductory study requisite to their most elementary understanding. But that is another matter—and the music of Bach and Handel will not be further discussed herein. The reader interested in increasing his understanding of its accentuation will be able to do so by combining the principles expounded in this survey with the excellent treatises available on eighteenth century interpretation.

However, with the other two leading eighteenth century masters, Haydn and Mozart, the situation is entirely different. Accents were among the regular equipment of their musical vocabularies; and their use of them is so consummate that from their scores alone one could not suspect that accents were then still quite a novelty on the musical scene.

But the sonata form, in which they did much of their most important work, was also a novelty; it had arisen, and grown, to the viable state in which they found it, in a very short time—about two decades. But it had done this by dint of the labors of many men, who had built the style of which it was a cardinal feature while the last great masters of the former style, the baroque, were finishing out their creative careers in voluntary isolation from it. Oddly enough, this new movement had as its leading figure a son of one of those masters—Carl Philip Emanuel Bach. The style which it had brought into being was the "style galant," the spirit of which involved the inclusion within a single movement of a variety of sentiments and effects. It sought after greater personal expression, flexibility, drama, and contrast. In place of a seemingly inexhaustible flow of serene sound, divided only into broad and stately terraces, there came drama, and a profusion of detailed emotion. When the performer of a baroque score glanced at its opening bars, he was presumed to perceive its general mood, and to know all he had to know about what to do; but the new music of the style galant required a greatly expanded palette of nuances, which no performer was expected to divine, and a running commentary of all sorts of directions. And notable among the new nuances were accents.

The prototype of one of the two main types of them appears in the works of Carl Philip Emanuel Bach, and is explained by him in his admirable and authoritative "Essay on the Art of Playing the Clavier." *
It consists of a vertical line above or below the note to which it applies,

* On page 154 of the American edition.

and signifies that the note is to be struck with a smart, detached stroke. In some printed editions this line is thickened at the end farther away from the note, and thus appears ▼ or ⬩. Clearly this is the ancestor of all the accent symbols that consist of letterless signs; and it is the only symbol to indicate anything in the nature of an accent that is found throughout Carl Philip Emanuel Bach's works, for orchestra as well as clavier. The other main type, that of *sf* and its compounds, was evidently completely unknown to him. It would be neat, simple and logical to ascribe that symbol to Italian origin, as it stands for an Italian term; but as we shall see, the Italian composers of the era we are discussing followed the same procedure as Carl Philip Emanuel Bach; and the earliest found users of the symbol *sf* were not Italian in any sense.

It is needless to point out the great importance of Carl Philip Emanuel Bach in the esteem of his contemporaries and immediate successors. Whenever Mozart, throughout his early life, mentioned "Bach," he meant Carl Philip Emanuel Bach; the son was obviously the arbiter of those times, and the "old man," when he was thought of at all, was considered a scholarly but peculiar and innocuous old fogy. Another son, J. C. Bach, had settled in London, and in England at that time "Bach" meant J. C. At any rate, Carl Philip Emanuel's influence was vast; and among the symphony composers of his period whose accenting procedure is exactly the same as his, are Reutter, Wagenseil, Schlöger, Boccherini, Starzer, Sammartini, Schwindl, Franzl, and Ditters. Another of them, Hurlebusch, wrote a device consisting of a whole note with two such marks above it—this must have been meant as equivalent to two half notes, each struck according to the symbol. And be it here noted that in the scores of all those composers, this accent symbol is found in all levels of dynamics.

The following composers used those same marks in the same way, but also occasionally made use of other symbols: L.A.T. Kozeluch, Gossec, J. Stamitz, Vanhall. Of these, Kozeluch is the only one to use the symbol >, which he does in all levels of dynamics, but never on the first beat of a bar—evidently he associated it with syncopations. He also uses *SF,* both alone and in conjunction with >; and *SF* is the symbol he chooses for the accentuation of chords whose musical function is expressive rather than explosive. With him, a *SF* does not affect the dynamics of the whole passage except for the note (usually participated in by all the instruments playing) to which it applies. Gossec's other symbol is *rinf;* it also does not affect ensuing dynamics. However, with Stamitz, this symbol, written "rinF," does make the ensuing dynamics *forte,* for he always indicates *p* to resume a previous level of *piano.* With Vanhall, *f* and *sf* are loosely equivalent; in the orchestral parts of his symphonies, at points where some instruments have *sf,* others whose space on the page is crowded have *f.* Sometimes his mark of *sfor* is followed by a *p,* sometimes by no mark until another *sfor.*

It clearly appears that there was a great want of agreement on the properties of accent symbols; many composers were not even clear about their own conceptions of them. But lest this seem a harsh judgment, it should be emphasized that in that time, symbols for different things *looked* so much alike that the things they stood for could easily be imagined as *being* much alike. It is hard to realize this without having passed through one's hands and before one's eyes a great many printed orchestral parts of the period (full scores were ordinarily not printed at all). In them one frequently finds, for instance, *forte* represented by *for,* and accents by *sfor,* both in the same kind of type and in the same relative position on the line. Mistakes were easy to make and easy to let pass; that is, even assuming that they were considered mistakes at all. This conclusion is strengthened by an examination of the scores of these composers, who abandoned the use of the Carl Philip Emanuel Bach symbol entirely and marked their accents with other symbols: Monn, Holzbaur, Christian Cannabich, Lord Kelly, Arne.

With Monn, *rinf* is rare, but on some of the chords on which it appears in some of the voices, *f* is the symbol used in other voices. And even when the dynamics are *piano, rinf* is always followed by a *p,* thus indicating that Monn considered it practically equivalent to *f.* Holzbaur's usage is similar except in that he always follows a *rinf* by either *p* or *f;* thus with him, *rinf* was a term of ambiguous meaning as to dynamics. Cannabich is also uncertain—he sometimes finds it ad-

visable to follow a *sf* in *piano* with a *p* on the next note. He also
writes puzzling combinations such as this:

This example also shows how the rigid convention of writing marks as
close as possible to the note, regardless of at what point they are to
take effect, produces not clarity but confusion. With Lord Kelly, *"for"*
stood either for *forte* or *sforzando*—one can tell only from the context,
and sometimes one has to deduce that from the next mark afterward;
and *"rinf"* is conceived by him to raise the ensuing dynamics, as does
the excellent Dr. Arne, for whenever it appears in *piano* he is scrupulous to follow it by a *p.*

And yet some composers, notably of the Mannheim school (though
as we have seen, not all of these either), thought their way through to
a clear distinction between accents and dynamics. Their scores show
without question that their accents apply to the designated notes only,
leaving the dynamic level unaffected. Besides Kozeluch and Gossec,
they include Richter and Eichner, whose symbol for accents was *rf,*
and Herschel, whose symbol was *sfor.* Jommelli used both the Carl
Philip Emanuel Bach symbol, on short notes, and *rinfort* on sustained
notes, even some that are slurred to their predecessors; yet, in some
piano passages he followed *rinfort* by *f,* showing that he clearly did
make the distinction.

We have briefly sketched the unsteady development of accents up to
the point at which the music that includes them, and which is still in
the living concert repertoire, began to be written. The earliest composer of such music thoroughly absorbed the resources he found before
him and fused them in the luminous crucible of his brilliant creative
faculty. His name was Franz Josef Haydn.

Illustrations of the music of Haydn and other composers will be
found starting on page 161.

THREE

HAYDN AND MOZART

Almost any one of Haydn's mature symphonies will serve excellently for an inquiry into his musical language, including his use of accents. However, his last and probably greatest symphony, the London, supplies a richer illustration than most of the others for the matters here considered; and let us now study the accents in it.

The symbols are of two kinds: *sf* and >. As Haydn was a painstaking craftsman, the question arises whether he might have meant different types of accents by each of the two symbols. However, this question can be instantly disposed of, and in the negative, by a glance at bars 145 and 159 of the *allegro* of the first movement, in which the different symbols are used with the same motive in passages of identical character—and the second bar of the second movement and the first bar of the minuet, in which the same symbol is used for two accents which cannot conceivably be of similar type. Nor can the use of the different symbols be accounted for by considerations of whether the accents occur on light or heavy beats—for both symbols are used on both, at different places. The conclusion is inescapable that the symbols Haydn used were to him thoroughly equivalent and interchangeable.

The *allegro* of the first movement begins quietly with the statement of a wonderful sixteen-bar theme, divided into four four-bar phrases. The statement of the theme is followed by a restatement, but a varied and expanded one, in a brilliant and energetic fortissimo by the full orchestra, with flashing drums and trumpets. *(Fig. 1)* When it reaches what was originally the beginning of the second four-bar phrase, in bar 24 of the *allegro,* the first note of the melody is prolonged; and the plunge into its B minor harmony, which previously has been unobtrusive, becomes dramatic. All these considerations lead to the inference that while the thematic material is basically identical, the character here is sharply contrasted with that of the previous statements. And to confirm this inference, the prolonged note, together with its sequel two bars later, is the first accented note in the symphony!

Now we must consider which type of accent to apply. Since the whole passage is *fortissimo,* it is extremely unlikely that the eighteenth century composer meant a still louder tone here; so it is reasonable to exclude the volume factor. And since the note is slurred to its successor, there exists no room for choice as to its duration. There remain to be considered the factors of initial "bite," or acute attack, and tone quality, or color. As to the former, all the indications mentioned call for it. And the intensity of the music at the spot of the accented notes demands an expressive tone color. The accent type, therefore, is 13.

The next accents are in bars 38 and 39 of the *allegro,* which are identical. At this point the brilliant restatement of the theme is past; the music has become discursive and is beginning to modulate to the second subject. *(Fig. 2)* The drums are silent; and the brass is subdued. The accented chord is a diminished seventh, a highly active and expressive chord, and it resolves into the minor mode; now everything implies a more pensive and "conversational" character than before. The melody is in the first violins alone. In their part, the dynamics and duration factors are excluded by the same data as in the preceding instance;

here one could reason that the "bite" factor should also be excluded, so as not to disturb the gradually calmer emotional content, leaving the accent one of color alone (type 22) if it were not for the fact that this accent occurs on the third quarter of the bar. This is the first time in the symphony that the first note of a bar is outweighed by a later note; and since the rhythmic propulsion is still continuing, uninterrupted since the beginning, it seems clear that the composer meant to make a point of this first rhythmic displacement. Such an effect would not be sufficiently brought out by type 22; therefore the violins should here also play type 13.

The fact that the continued rhythmic propulsion must be clearly taken into account here is shown by an effect in the next bar, 40, which will fail if the rhythmic propulsion is allowed to weaken before it. In that bar there occurs another rhythmic displacement, but a still greater one than the preceding—a true syncopation—for here it occurs on the second quarter-note of the bar! And it also carries an accent. The melody note is a half-note; otherwise all the notes and dynamics of the second quarter are the same as those of the first quarter. Therefore, the significance of this accent is rhythmic and melodic, not harmonic; and since this last element of this accent is lacking, the accent, if it is to be of no lesser amplitude than the preceding ones, must have another factor in addition to those of the preceding ones. This additional factor is indeed available, that of duration, since the accented note is not tied to its successor. The lengthening factor, therefore, should be applied here, by sustaining the accented note for its full value and sounding its successor with a quick change of bow, without allowing the bow to either stop moving or leave the string. The accent is type 14; and it should be helped by playing the note before it with somewhat more shortness and lightness than normal.

Now let us return to bars 38-39. There, as regards the rest of the orchestra, the oboes and other strings have a steady succession of eighth-notes on the supporting harmony, and the other winds have harmony in half-notes. The first violins play two quarter-notes beginning at the accented note. This combination poses an additional problem: how long is the intended duration of the accent, and is it the same for the whole orchestra? If it applies to only one note, is that note the flutes' half-note, the first violins' quarter-note, and/or the basses' eighth-note? And in which parts, if any, does it apply to more, or to less, than one complete note?

On studying the first violin part, the principal voice here, it becomes clear that if the accent were imparted to both notes, the resulting phrasing would be stiff and ugly, and besides, it would not give the effect which the composer seems to have intended, namely, of emphasizing the incidence of a strong discord on a weak beat. Therefore the accent will apply to only the first note, and its duration in the first violin part will accordingly be one quarter's. How does this conclusion affect the accent of the rest of the orchestra? Since the passage is decidedly homophonic, the melody is the controlling determinant—the *primus inter pares* at the very least—therefore the other voices must adjust themselves to the first violin part. Those that have half-notes should attack with a "bite" and sustain with intensified tone color for one quarter's duration, and play the remaining quarter's value of the tone as if it were unaccented—type 13; and those that play the eighth-notes should support the melody by accenting *two* notes: the one occurring on the accented beat and the one immediately following it. Both notes should be played with a heavier tone and sustained for their full value (thus differing from their neighbors); and besides, the first one should have a "bite." So, the first of the eighth-notes will be accented with type 14, and the second with type 23. The whole orchestra is now accounted for, effectuating the written accent in conformity with the context of the music at this point.

The next accent to be dealt with here occurs in bars 88 and 90 of the same *allegro*. It is at the beginning of a two-bar phrase which is repeated; and it is marked with the symbol >. Here the theme is in the dominant key; the place is near the end of the exposition. *(Fig. 3)* The same theme recurs in the tonic near the end of the recapitulation, and with the same accent mark. Its occurrence in both places is *piano,* preceded by five bars of *piano*. The chord is the minor subdominant—a sudden shadow—after a long stretch of unclouded tonic-and-dominant. While the rhythmic propulsion prevalent in this movement might admit of an acute attack here, the gently melancholy mood here has the better of it, and makes an acute attack out of place. The color factor should surely be present, as should the volume factor if, as it always should be, kept to the minimum. The natural musical phrasing of this melodic passage would suggest a slight dynamic stress on the accented note even if it were not accented. This accent, then, is of type 25. Another possibility, however, which the context would allow, is an accent of class C—and it should be very beautiful. In such a case the dynamics factor would take the form of a *crescendo-diminuendo* on the accented note, or even over the whole bar. Or a class C accent (it would have to be type 36) could be combined with, say, one of type 6, forming a compound accent of class D.

The remaining accents in the first movement need no further discussion.

The slow movement is as remarkable for its economy of material as for its profound and subtle sentiment. Its first five chords are: tonic, dominant, submediant, subdominant, dominant seventh in the third inversion. *(Fig. 4)* The fourth of these carries an accent (marked *sf*), which prepares the poignant harmonic progression to the fifth chord, accompanying a fall of a seventh in the melody. By this accent the composer did not mean a purely dynamic emphasis—for when he meant just that, he showed it very clearly in bars 27 and 29 of this movement, where he marked two notes *f,* each followed by *p*. Nor, after the quiet deceptive resolution, on the third chord, of the dominant preceding it, is an "acute" attack conceivable. Therefore the accent intended is one of color, an intense and warmly expressive tone, with a slightly increased volume—type 25. And when the next tone is reached, an abrupt cessation of the accent tone must not be made—there should be a *"diminuendo* of tone" into it. One's own ear, taste, and thought should be sufficient authority for this interpretation; however, we have Haydn's own indication besides. For in later appearances of this theme, in which the long melody notes are broken up into scales in triplets (bars 99 and 123), the beat originally marked *sf* is marked *rf* with a *diminuendo* into the next beat; and this clearly shows the composer's conception of the accentuation of his theme in any guise.

Haydn's minuets are sturdy things, and one need not be too refined about their accents. The latter will generally be found to be adequately interpreted by types 2 and 10.

In the *finale* there are two accents that deserve special notice. The fourth bar of the first theme consists of two half-notes, the second one a whole tone above the first. *(Fig. 5)* Soon in the course of the movement this second note acquires an accent which is inseparable from it thenceforth. *(Fig. 6)* Thus the accent, similarly to a note, acquires an "ego" of its own. Being as it is on the weaker of the two beats of the bar, in an energetic movement, it should have type 14, the "color" to be imparted being one of sudden sobriety rather than excitement, like a "dead step" in an animated dance, and the effect of the accent will be enhanced by an absence of vibrato on the accented note. Now the point is this: at the end of the movement the composer writes this two-note motive, including its "me too" accent—but this time, and this time only, he displaces it by one beat, so that the accented note falls, at long last, on not the weak beat of the bar, but the strong one. *(Fig. 6)* This time the "color" can well be one of intensity, with good vibrato and sustained quality, as well as volume (type 17). The next two chords, which conclude the symphony, are marked simply *ff*—which, constituting merely the final cadence, are not thematic, and should be sounded with only normal *ff* strength, without the extra quality of the accented beat.

The other noteworthy accent occurs three times in the course of the second subject (the theme beginning at bars 84, 167, and 247)—assuredly one of the tenderest utterances ever penned in music. These accents lift the theme to its climax, and on their interpretation the quiet and sensitive beauty of the music largely depends. Firstly, a "bite" would be totally out of character and must be avoided. Secondly, all the accented notes are upbeats, in a highly flowing passage; their duration must be their full value. Thirdly, their color should be such as to confirm the searching character of the theme. Fourthly, a slight dynamic pressure would also be appropriate, as some would in all good musicianship be imparted even if there were no accent—but no earthly "bump" must be allowed to intrude into this heavenly strain. With all these factors, the accent indicated is type 26, with the full dynamic stress of the accent applied after rather than at the very inception of the tone, for, if applied fully at the very inception of the tone, it would impair the serenity of the theme.

It is hoped that on the principles indicated herein, the interpreter will be equipped to properly interpret Haydn's orchestral accents for himself.

As we now pass on to Mozart, the great overture to *The Magic Flute* will serve as an excellent guide to that master's accents. The first accent is encountered in the fifth bar; and the considerations as to its interpretation are as follows. While this music is not tragic, it is yet as solemn and monumental as any that Mozart ever wrote. The over-all mood is both noble and tender, and any suggestions of either energy or tension will impair it. The score at this point is marked thus: the violins and violas have *sf* on a quarter note tied over from the previous bar—the first example in this survey of such a device, and a rare one in musical literature (to realize its specially orchestral significance, try to imagine it in a score for the piano!). The timpani have one note, also *sf;* all the other instruments, some of which enter after a rest, others of which hold a long note that is part of a sustained melodic line, have *sfp*. The chord of this bar, as well as the preceding one, is the subdominant with an "added sixth." The tempo is slow, the dynamics *piano. (Fig. 8)*

The fact that the accent of part of the orchestra lies on a note that is tied over—it having originated at a previous point and being sustained *through* the accented beat—itself shows that the accent cannot be acute. This finding is confirmed by the music's mood. As to the accent's duration, the facts that the winds have *sfp* and the violins and violas *sf* on one quarter note show that the accent was intended to sound for no more than a quarter's duration. Whether it is to sound for a shorter duration than that will depend on the conductor's taste; however, a greater sense of majesty is attained by sustaining it to the limit. The one timpani note is not a sufficiently dominating element of the score to be considered as determining the accent's duration; it just marks the accented tone's inception. As to its further significance, it could conceivably mean a loud beat in the midst of soft, solemn music, but to so interpret it would oppose all other accessible indications. Also, if it were meant to be smartly struck, even softly, it would thereby be at variance with the remainder of the orchestra; and it may here be asserted as a rule that unless the evidence is clearly to the contrary, all simultaneous accents, in all instruments, at any point of an orchestral score, must be effectuated so as to contribute to, and produce, a consistent and unified result. The remaining possible interpretation of the timpani beat consists of an oblique, glancing stroke of the drumstick, which minimizes the percussive impression and emphasizes that of depth, resonance, and mystery. Considering the score as a whole, consistently with the method pursued in this survey, it appears that this last is the effect intended by the composer; and it also provides an additional key to the interpretation of the accents in the remainder of the orchestra; namely, that color is the predominant element of this accent—this is an accent primarily of stationary sound, as opposed to one of melody in motion. It must begin at the beginning of the tone, because of the timpani beat and the entrance of some instruments, but with great smoothness, and a tone of splendor and serenity. The volume factor, if present at all, should be so in only the slightest degree; in the conductor's discretion it can be entirely eliminated, since the brass and percussion entrance is itself a dynamic circumstance. Besides, the trombones are among the instruments that have rests immediately preceding the accented note; and Mozart was prominent among the classical composers whose use of trombones virtually invariably indicates a special effect, of majesty, terror, etc.

A further clarifying word on duration is needed here. Duration is involved, where there is an accent on a note with some sustained value, in two ways: one, in respect to its influencing the duration of the note itself; and two, in respect to how large a part of the duration of the note is affected with the accent, regardless of the duration of the note itself. In the instance we are considering, it is only the second sense in which duration is involved—because, to put it in one of several possible ways, any permissible amount of lengthening or shortening of any of the accented notes themselves would still have no effect on the expressive content of any of them; they are quite long already; and as for the second violins, the separation between the first and second quarters must be clearly heard, so a lengthening of the accented note there would be decidedly undesirable. The accented part of the note is determined by these considerations, which apply also to the similar accent in the second bar following. And the accent type will be 22 or 25.

The problem of the last three bars of the introduction should be distinguished from the one just discussed. Here, the *mfp* of the trombones clearly indicates a climactic height of the dynamics, greater than any heard hitherto since the fourth bar. *(Fig. 9)* The reason why the clarinets and horns have *sfp* here, instead of *mfp* like the trombones, is not obvious. One can take one's choice of two alternatives, each with its own line of reasoning. One is, that Mozart here wanted a single unified effect produced by all the instruments of the orchestra that are playing —an effect of a *mezzo-forte* chord, dropping to *piano,* with some kind of initial emphasis, yet not such a strong one that the trombones could safely be trusted to share in it. The clarinets and horns, being co-operative and not dictatorial instruments, are just right for providing a tone with a pleasant "leading edge" that is noticeable without being disproportionately keen. And while the trombones' *MFP* does not apply to the clarinets and horns, it still must be considered in deciding the type and also the quantity of accent the clarinets and horns are to have. That the composer here wanted a coloristic effect is obvious from the observation not so much of which instruments he included in his scoring, as of those which he left out. While the flutes, oboes, trumpets, and drums —all the instruments capable of a "bite" and a piercing tone—and the bassoons as well, all have notes available for both these chords, they are all silent. Mozart, therefore, must have wanted an open, dark, rich sound, emphatically without a "bite"; and, moreover, a sound consisting not of the combination of the separate timbres of the different instruments producing it, but of one homogeneous, velvety, sonorous wind-instrument chord.

While the half-note should be sustained for its full value, the duration of the accented part of it must be long enough, and only long enough, under the acoustic conditions of each performance, to allow the accent to effectuate itself; since the accent lacks the "bite," its presence will not be as instantly perceived as it would be if it had a "bite," and a little time must be allowed for the elements present in it to "sink in." And the *p*'s in the *mfp* and the *sfp* must commence simultaneously—the duration of the *mf* and the *sf* must be exactly the same. Each part of the chord affords a delicate problem in balance. In the first *mf* and *sf* part, the clarinets and horns can avoid being overcome by the trombones only by contributing their full instrumental and expressive color, as well as by matching them in volume; in the second part, it is rather the responsibility of the trombones to drop their tone sharply so as to allow the others to continue to blend with them on an equal footing. The accent, then, should be type 26.

The other line of reasoning argues that had Mozart meant an effect other than of the trombones standing out *"en dehors"*—the usual one with him—he would surely have surrounded them with a far greater array of other instruments than he did here, as he normally does in the rare spots where his trombones are manifestly intended to be a blending part of the whole. If his economical scoring here had been carefully calculated to highlight the sound of the trombones, with the remainder of the orchestra performing a purely supporting and subordinate role, he could hardly have scored it more admirably and unmistakably than he did here. Plausibility is added to this reasoning by the fact that the trombones all play different notes of the chord, thereby being self-sufficient, and the fact that the clarinets merely take over the top melodic line from the strings. According to this interpretation, only enough tone should be added to the clarinets and horns, on the *sf* part of their *sfp,* to gently "color" their assumption of the strings' tones, and the sonority of these wind chords is a bipartite one, with the trombones standing out and the other instruments merely forming a background; and the accent type, for the accented instruments, is 23. The reader can choose either of these solutions. The rule of a unified accent, formulated above, is not applicable, since the mark on the trombone parts is not an accent.

In bars 7-8-9-10 and similarly figured bars of the fugal opening of the *allegro, sfp*'s occur on sustained tones which are consonant at their inception, but which become suspensions by reason of harmonic motion around them, and then duly resolve. *(Fig. 9)* An acute attack on those tones would fit the tripping nature of the theme to which the accented notes are a counterpoint—as well as with a narrowly literal reading of the markings. However, a less incisive and more gently expressive rendition of the accent would do fuller justice to this wonderful music. Mozart is par excellence the maker of ethereal melodies, which soar on to their conclusions with effortless serenity. And it is in this character rather than that of his perky "cuteness" that he should be regarded here, particularly because of the plane of the opera—and, indeed, the overture alone—as a whole. No violence would be done to the written symbols by such an interpretation—in fact, they would be only the more fully respected thereby—for as has been shown, not only does *sf* not necessarily require an acute attack, but also in an *sfp* the exact point at which the *p* begins is not rigidly prescribed, nor whether it begins abruptly or by *diminuendo*. Musically speaking, too, a suspension should assert itself most conspicuously at the instant at which it becomes dissonant. Therefore it appears that here, while an acute type would not be incorrect, any other type would be preferable, even one from class C, such as a familiar *crescendo-diminuendo*.

However, beginning with the first *forte* in the *allegro,* the music takes on the character of combined grandeur and nervous excitement so typical of Mozart's later tuttis. The accented notes on the second quarter of the bar, which occur frequently, are both energetic and melodic (since even when they are not, technically speaking, suspensions, they behave like suspensions, descending stepwise as they do on the fourth quarter of the bar); therefore while some expressive color is called for, an acute attack will increase their contribution to the musical whole. Type 13, then, is indicated. *(Fig. 10)*

A final word of caution should be said about the trombones in the sixth, seventh, and eighth bars before the end. The entire orchestra in these three bars is *piano,* having become so quite suddenly and unexpectedly; and especially since the *piano* is not marked in the trombonists' parts, the sudden *piano* ordinarily catches the trombonists by surprise; in fact, they are usually even totally unaware of it. *(Fig. 11)* Conductors should instruct them to make their accent a soft, round, and noble one, something quite different from the blare usually heard here, and in keeping with the sudden hush that comes over the hubbub.

It is hoped that enough has been said to constitute some guide to the accents of Mozart's last and greatest manner. However, since the works of this class are much less numerous than his earlier ones, which with all their grace and perfection do not compass the majesty and profundity of his last ones, an example from his earlier ones is here in order, *viz.* the "Haffner" symphony, K. 385.

The first accents encountered in the first movement occur toward the end of the second subject, in the rising passage of measured trills. The symbol is *sf,* at the beginning of each trilled note, each of which is preceded by a detached sixteenth note—which in the *alla breve* tempo is the shortest value that can be articulated with clarity. The dynamics are *forte. (Fig. 12)* All this data indicates that the character is brilliance and energy, and that the purpose of the accent is to intensify that character. Therefore this accent must be "acute." As to its other factors, if the effect of the accent were to continue past the point of its inception, the dynamics would sound *ff* instead of the indicated *f,* and the intensified sound throughout the orchestra would thicken the texture so as to thwart the best effect of the passage. At last, then, an accent has been encountered which could be type 1! And if the orchestra is a large one, it should be that, or else type 3 (the color being bright), as 2 or 4 would probably make too heavy a sound. However, with a small orchestra, the type should be 2 or 4.

In the second and fourth bars following the peak of that ascent, another *sf,* on the second (*alla breve*) beat, is encountered. *(Fig. 12)* Significantly, it is marked only in the melodic parts, not in the supporting parts. Evidently the composer wanted not a collective thump on that beat but just a sprightly melodic line. Moreover, the same melodic parts, at the beginning of the present theme, are marked *"stacc."* When we consider all these data together with the accent, what is our conclusion? Let us suppose the *"stacc."* applying also to the accented note; is it not obvious that this is an impossibility? For the accented tone is that on which the whole phrase "sits down," and it wants to sing into its successor. Hence the accent must have the lengthening factor. Also the energetic character demands an acute attack. And the importance of the accented note in the melodic curve justifies its having greater intensity than its companions; this, too, will give the illusion—which will suffice and should not be made explicit—of a higher dynamic level than its companions', which, being *staccato,* do not have the opportunity to achieve a substantial sonority. Therefore this accent is of type 14.

The only other accent in this symphony calling for special notice is that in the second bar of the second movement. *(Fig. 13)* The phrase is in *piano,* and of four bars' length. The winds supporting the melody of the first violins sustain the harmony throughout the bar, with the symbol *sfp.* The violas, celli, and basses have only a quarter note, *sf.* The second violins, playing a conventional *staccato* arpeggiated figure, have no symbol at all. Here the tempo being *andante,* and the mood leisurely, there is no reason for an acute accent. One can confidently be satisfied that this accent is simply expressive, to intensify the longest and highest note in the phrase. In fact, this accent could be one of class C if it were not that the winds have *sfp,* indicating that the accented portion of the tone is to be at the tone's inception. One more detail remains to be noted, and that is, that as in the introduction to the *Magic Flute* overture, one member of the orchestra—here the first bassoon—has the *sfp* on a note tied over from the preceding bar; and thus the accent cannot possibly be "acute." Melodic considerations require the effect of the accent to extend beyond the starting point of the tone, effectuated by color, and, in the conductor's choice, volume also —type 22 or 25. The duration of the accented portion is also in the conductor's discretion. One additional feature to be observed here is that in the lower strings, the accented quarter note of the second bar will naturally and ordinarily be sustained for a greater duration than the unaccented quarter-note of the first bar; therefore for that section of the orchestra the accent is type 23 or 26.

It remains to point out a few more examples of Mozart's reasoning about the shorthand symbol *sf.* They are to be found in his *Serenade for Wind Instruments, K. 375.* At the very opening, this symbol, without any other marking, appears over the first chord, which is sustained throughout the bar. *(Fig. 14)* In the second bar *sfp* appears over the first of the three chords in the bar. Thus far not a single dynamic indication louder than *p* has been given. But when we reach the third chord, we find it marked *fp.* Would it not be absurd to play the first two chords, sonorous as they are, softly, and then open up into *forte* on just the third? Therefore, considering the context, the conclusion is easily reached that, by the *sf* on the first two chords Mozart meant *f sf.* This conclusion is confirmed by the beginning of the recapitulation of this movement, where the same music is repeated literally, *following a crescendo.* Lest it seem to be laboring the obvious to reason out this point, let the reader be reminded that this survey is based on the thesis, well supported in musical literature, that an accent does not necessarily involve either loudness or acuteness, despite the misconception, frequently maintained, that it does; therefore instances where the results seem to support the misconception should be explained, if anything, even more carefully than those where the results disprove it.

The eternal verities are not adumbrated in this piece; it is, in fact, notwithstanding its touches of sentiment, one of Mozart's decidedly lighter and occasional works. A chord similar to the opening one of this work, if found in, say, *Don Giovanni* or one of the later symphonies, might well call for a plain accent, to project the sense of depth or the transcendental. But here, where care is tossed to the winds, another atmosphere is in order, that of festivity; and festivity begins with an acute accent. Better yet if the extra significance, which the accent symbol shows should be imparted to these first chords, includes the lengthening factor, as well as that of color. Therefore for the first accent we have type 17; and for the next (*sfp*), type 4. (Interestingly enough, while here Mozart makes the symbol *sf* do double duty for "accent" and *"forte,"* Beethoven, as will be shown, sometimes does just the opposite—he makes *f* stand for "accent"!)

This movement is also noteworthy for containing a fairly clear example of a class C accent—in bar 214, or the twenty-fifth before the end. *(Fig. 15)* Formally considered, that bar introduces the coda, giving a pathetic new turn to a progression previously heard at the close of the exposition. It is occupied entirely by a diminished seventh chord which leads from a D flat major triad to an F minor triad. The "unexpected-inevitable" feature here is not so much this diminished seventh, surprising and dissonant as it is, but the quiet minor chord to which it resolves. And this resolution is made more poignant and satisfying by an intensification of the dissonant chord that resolves into it. This, then, is the function of the *sf* on the resolving chord, and its sole discernible reason for being. How, then, to inflect this chord to effect that purpose? By a stress on its inception? No, as that would damage the unity of the melodic progression. Also, an unvaried tone, sustained uniformly throughout the chord's duration, of no matter what color, will not do the trick. It is clear that this chord needs a stress for no more than part of its duration somewhere between its inception and its termination, and thus what is required is a class C accent. Since the chord is not slurred to its successor, and the two must be closely linked, it demands also the lengthening factor. So the type of accent needed here is 37.

Mozart surely is in that small company of "perhaps the greatest of them all"; and nothing shows his vast musicianship more clearly than the almost bewildering variety of his use of accents. This, however, can be systematized, and reduced to order, by a patient and rational approach to his methods such as that indicated herein.

FOUR

BEETHOVEN

Beethoven is the true and worthy successor of Haydn and Mozart in that he not only mastered those elements of their styles which his genius could put to good use, but also added much of his own. While he sang of gods and peasants both, as they did, each in his own way, he also broadened and clarified the human content of music and made it express values, not necessarily more sublime or profound, but more diverse and familiar than its scope had previously been considered. He exuded a humor, an earthy affirmation, and a powerful personal utterance beside which the music of the eighteenth century, with all its brilliance and sophistication, seems pale. Whereas before him the various instruments of the orchestra had acquired character, he endowed them with personality. He enriched objective perfection with humanity and universal truth. And while his method is occasionally that of suggestion, it is ordinarily one of forthright and explicit assertion.

33

45250 BRIAR CLIFF COLLEGE LIBRARY SIOUX CITY, IOWA

It is but natural, therefore, that his music should show a great free-dom and variety in its use of all resources, including accents. His accents will be examined in two examples: the *Eighth Symphony,* whose beauties are more those of form than of content, and the *Ninth Symphony,* a mighty spiritual document, and probably the crowning achievement of his entire creative career.

The first accent in the *Eighth Symphony* appears in bar 28 shortly before the pause preceding the second subject of the first movement. The tempo is *allegro,* the dynamics *forte,* the time signature three-four. *(Fig. 16)* The accent, symbolized *sf,* is on the third quarter of every one of four successive bars, all on the chord of B flat seventh, second inver-sion. The musical underlying considerations for the accent seem to be that from the beginning of the work to this point, the pulse has been "three-square"; the stress is now shifted to the third quarter to counter-act the possible monotony and to readjust the hearer's rhythmic sense in preparation for the unusually graceful second subject. Moreover one can validly discover an expressive element in these accents, inasmuch as the first two accented notes, with their successors, constitute compres-sions into one quarter's space of the motive which extends over the whole previous bar. And according to the law of nature, when some-thing is squeezed, it results in a mass with the same weight and quan-tity of matter as before occupying a smaller space. What it loses in space it gains in density—compactness and strength. Thus the motive, as it loses space, duly gains compression and force; and the law of nature is satisfied.

Now these accents should have the acute factor because of the char-acter of the music (as in the *allegro* of the Haydn symphony discussed above); volume, too, according to Beethoven's vigorous style, espe-cially as the prevailing dynamic level is just *f.* As to the other factors —if the interpreter means to emphasize the thematic unity of the motive with the preceding bars, he will "melodize" the accented note—make it long, and color it expressively. In such a case the accent will be type 17. But if he wishes to emphasize the rhythmic element as well as clarify the written texture, he will direct the players to slightly *shorten* the accented note; thus the type will be 12. In both these cases the accent will not apply to the second violins and violas, who are scrubbing away too hard to do any more than take the down-bowed accented note and its repetition with a type 2 or 6 stroke.

The last two accents present a slightly different situation; because if their effect is to shorten their notes, and the note that follows each one played as written, the accent will have a much reduced effect in displacing the normal stresses within each bar; so, here the accent must lengthen its note, and it would further its effect to slightly lighten the unaccented note following each accented one. The accent will be type 11.

Most of the other accents in this movement present no problem, being acute with a dynamics factor and, where clearly appropriate, the lengthening factor as well. There is no exceptional subtlety in their use—they are merely one of the resources of Beethoven's muscular idiom. In the unique second movement, the accents, all occurring as they do on long tones in the melodies, and in *forte,* call for factors of color and lengthening in addition to the "bite"—excepting that in a highly lyrical conception the latter should be absent—thus they would be type 14 or 23.

The third movement furnishes examples of further uses to which accents can be put. At the very beginning, the purpose of the accents is to clarify and establish the rhythm. The upbeat to the first bar is identical with its first and second beats, with the sole difference that the upbeat is not accented and the other beats are. *(Fig. 17)* This slight but essential detail, if properly observed in performance, enables the hearer immediately to orient himself as to the location of the bar-line. While the mood does not call for color in the accented tones, it does call for a "bite" wherever possible—that is, on notes which are not slurred to their predecessors; type 2 or 10 should be used. Where the accented notes are so slurred, the type should be 5 or 19.

This movement also contains a motive of which an accent is an integral part (as in the finale of the Haydn symphony discussed above). This motive consists of but two notes: an eighth-note, an eighth-rest, and a long note a fourth higher. Such an embryonic "germ" needs some further element to give it interest, and the *sf,* invariably found on its second note, fully suffices. The motive first appears in the trumpets at the beginning of the movement *(Fig. 17),* and grows in significance until it has the orchestra all to itself for a few bars in a stretto-like culmination. *(Fig. 18)* And no matter which beat of the bar it falls on, the *sf* is always on the second note. Since the accented tone is always sustained (except of course in the timpani), and the motive is essentially so trivial, it seems that something larger than a class A accent is required. But neither the emotional content of the movement nor the character of this motive admit of the application of sufficient expressive color to effectuate the accent without still additional factors; and the long tone, if sustained with added dynamic force, would tend to pass beyond the realm of emphasis into that of ugliness. Therefore, what shall the solution be? The accent should be effectuated with, firstly, an acute attack; to this attack should be added the slightest degree of extra dynamic force, which should be sustained for a brief instant after the attack; the extra dynamic force should then disappear, the remainder of the tone being held to the end with intensified color alone, and its end should not come before the expiration of its full value. The type of the accent would thus be 17—with the variation that the dynamics factor is present only at the tone's inception and briefly thereafter, not for the tone's full duration. Hence this accent, schematically considered, strictly falls among those grouped into class E.

Incidentally, in the stretto-like culmination, the first note of the entrance of the motive in the woodwinds is usually not heard because of its shortness and the accent on the next note. Thus one who does not know the score does not know what the long accented note is doing up there, or where it came from. Therefore in this entrance, care should be taken that the first note be clearly heard.

Similar considerations apply to the accents in the development section of the *finale,* and to those in the last few pages of the symphony. As to the *finale,* one might also speculate as to why Beethoven did *not* accent even one of those roaring C sharps (the first of which occurs in bar 17) which burst in on the music always when it has sunk down to its quietest, and which probably are the most conspicuous feature of this movement. Their object is a sudden and violent destruction, for the time being, of the melody, the harmony, and the rhythm of the surrounding music; and they certainly succeed in this object. Surely they would seem to be natural subjects of an accent; yet they are marked just *ff.* The answer is probably found in the fact that on every occasion of their intrusion in which the dynamic plane does not immediately thereafter return to *pp,* the following music bears the mark *sempre ff.* Evidently the composer wanted to make sure that the C sharp would be sustained without any drop in its force throughout its duration; and he supposed, with much reason, that if he had added a *sf* to the *ff,* some of his interpreters would misunderstand his intentions so as to allow a drop in the force of the tone at some point prior to its termination.

There is certainly no need here to describe Beethoven's Eighth and Ninth symphonies either as wholes or in details. However, for the sake of this survey let it be pointed out that the Eighth, admirable as it is in its invention, fancy, and musical mastery, and power of making a good deal out of fairly inconsequential material, is yet clearly a minor work, in which matters of weighty import do not figure substantially, nor does it tug very insistently at any heart strings. But the Ninth is a different matter entirely; in it the subject matter is everything, and vast and momentous it is indeed. The pundits and public may argue *ad infinitum* as to whether it "comes off"; here, the question of whether it is triumphantly successful is irrelevant. What matters here, as to which there can be no dispute worth mentioning, is that masterly efforts at expressing great and beautiful values are in progress, and to a large extent they are magnificently successful.

This is obvious at once, as the mysterious opening suggests vast spaces, "where the morning stars sang together." It soon builds up to a mighty outburst of the main theme, by the entire orchestra in bare octaves. In the fifth bar of the theme, two things make their first appearance in the symphony: a chord, and an accent. Throughout his creative career Beethoven was obsessed by the elemental tonic-dominant relationship, and he widely exploited its potentialities. To him it stood for something like the ultimate in meaning, beauty, and power; it had transcendental, mystical implications. Knowing this, one can more fully appreciate this fifth bar and its successor. The time signature is two-four, the dynamics *forte.* The fourth bar consists of four unisons on the bare notes of the dominant chord; so that the tonic unison on the first beat of the fifth bar sounds cadential. But the second beat bears a dominant chord; and the first beat of the next bar, a full tonic chord. The two chords are orchestrated as fully as possible, even with complete chords in the violins. They, and the bare tonic which preceded them, are marked *sf*. There is nothing but silence in the sixth bar, after the tonic chord; here, then, is the true cadence of this phrase, which is so emphasized by the *sf*'s. Further, the fifth bar is the first bar of the theme in which the second beat is felt to be of equal weight to the first. All the notes of the fifth and sixth bars are dotted eighths with sixteenth-rests between—a meticulousness of notation rarely encountered before a much later date. *(Fig. 19)*

Considering all these data, it is clear that in the scheme of this composition these chords are no mere conventional cadence, but a creative figure packed with emotional significance. The composer wanted them played heavily, long, and with intensity, and yet distinctly separated from one another. Accents of type 17 seem best suited to these chords, as well as to all that follow, as far as the first change of key-signature. At that point the main theme of the second subject begins—a quiet four-bar phrase, the pattern of which is identical in each bar: a dotted quarter followed by an eighth, a fourth or fifth higher; and the first note of each bar is higher than that of the preceding bar. And every eighth-note of this theme is accented. The dynamics are *piano. (Fig. 20)*

If one were to apply the same type of accent here as in the preceding section, the result would be a series of rather amusing thumps—which might well fit in the *Eighth Symphony,* but which would be most inappropriate here. For one thing, while in the preceding section the accents fell generally on the longer notes and on the principal beats, here all the accents are on the short notes and on light beats—increasing the already obvious contrast from the preceding material. This melody is a noble, flowing, and contemplative one—or at least it should be thus performed in order to remain in the exalted frame of the symphony. The accents in it, therefore, should be plain and should lack the dynamics factor, intensity being afforded by color alone. The absence of a "bite," indicated by the musical character, is supported by the fact that, while the statement of the theme contains no slurs, the re-statement, which occurs immediately with a slight alteration, has a slur extending over each bar. Here, surely, a "bite" on the eighth-note is impossible; and this, if nothing else, should indicate the phrasing, accentuation, and the composer's conception of the original statement. The often reliable maxim that the inclusion of one detail in one statement and its exclusion from another indicates an intended contrast in that respect between the two does not apply here, because there is nothing in the musical context to suggest that a contrast is intended between the character of the statement and that of the restatement; in fact, the shortness of the theme allows no time for a contrast to intervene, and standard musical procedure, which Beethoven follows here because it serves his purpose, ordinarily prescribes a repetition of a theme, without any thought of contrast, at such points as this.

Now as regards the lengthening factor, simple analysis shows each eighth-note to belong, not to the dotted quarter which precedes it, but to that which follows it. Therefore if the lengthening factor is absent, this connection will probably not be manifested in performance. The accent type, accordingly, should be 23.

This conclusion suggests the paradoxical reflection that in order to achieve consistency in the large, it is sometimes necessary to be inconsistent in the smaller matters. For if the accents applied up to this point were similar, the spiritual unity of the symphony would already have been broken. Contrasting material must contrast in texture but not in inherent spirit. And differing textures within the same spiritual frame may have to be differently interpreted in order to maintain the underlying homogeneity between them.

Finally, it must be mentioned that the symbol for this series of accents is not *sf* but $>$. The simplest possible explanation of this piece of evidence seems to be also the right one: viz, that Beethoven meant to indicate a different quality of intensity here from that which he wanted in the previous material, and thus used a different symbol. That he felt differently about the two symbols can be deduced from an examination of his other works, in which one sees that he usually uses *sf,* and reserves $>$ for the quiet inward passages. Significantly enough, there is not a single $>$ in the entire *Eighth Symphony*. This explanation confirms the submitted analysis of this symphony's accents thus far, but at the apparent expense of the general principle of this survey, *viz.* that the symbol chosen has nothing to do with the type of accent. However, it is a poor rule that has not so much as a single exception; in fact, it may be taken as a confirmation of the rule, that the exception is, of all the great composers, the most uncouth. Furthermore, one can easily condone Beethoven, in his ferocious search for all possible means for achieving his ends, for resorting to devices which have turned out to be unnecessary.

One more set of accents in the first movement remains to be noted. It occurs in the last bars of *fortissimo* in the exposition. The cadence motive, with a rhythm of tum-te-tah, is treated in imitation between the violins and nearly everybody else. *(Fig. 21)* In the first three bars, the "everybody else" have a *sf* on the "tah"; but the violins have the *sf* on the "tah" of only the third bar, while in the first two they have instead merely *f*. Now the last dynamic mark before the beginning of the tum-te-tah's is *ff*. Can it have been Beethoven's intention that the violins' "tah's" should be *less* loud than their "tum-te's" and their neighbors' "tum-te-tah's"? Any answer other than No would lead to an absurdity, to which any rational solution, even if specially invented, is to be preferred. The only rational solution that presents itself here is simply that these *f*'s are rough symbols for accents, equivalent to the *sf*'s of the "everybody else." A glance at the corresponding spot in the recapitulation will confirm this solution, for there the violins have *sf*. As with the first subject, all the accents should be of type 17.

A few bars later the "tum-te-tah" figure falls in pitch over a space of four bars, and every "tah" is marked with both an *f* and a *staccato* dot. Here, as before, one must assume the *f*'s to stand for *sf*'s. But taking them together with the dots opens the situation to differing interpretations. One can (A) take the *staccato* dots to be a mere caution against excessive prolongation of the note because of the accent, so that it will be sure not to sound as if tied to its successor; one can (B) take them to indicate a shortening accent, such as type 12 or 18; or one can (C) interpret them as one often would in Brahms, that is, as indicating weight to be applied to the note. Probably a combination of (A) and (C) would be the solution most helpful to the music; the duration factor being not involved at all, but extra dynamic force and weight being applied to the accented tones. The accent would thus be type 16; or if the "bite" is not to the interpreter's taste, then 25.

The same idiosyncrasy—*f* standing for *sf*—is encountered at many points in the second movement. As the *scherzando* character of the movement would be impaired by any lengthening of the notes, the accents should be type 1 or 2. It must be admitted that the problem of the first six bars is not free from obscurity. *(Fig. 22)* Those bars would certainly seem explosive enough without extra expenditure of force. One can only gather that the composer felt the necessity of special emphasis on the first notes of the third and fifth bars because they are the ones that spell out the tonality.

In the third movement, which is the slow one, accents are found in only four bars; and as they are clearly of two different types, occurring in pairs of bars, they will be thus discussed. The first pair of bars is in the second variation, in twelve-eight time, of the main theme; and the bars in which the accents are found are the seventh *(Fig. 23)* and eleventh *(Fig. 24),* in the florid first violin part. Similarly, as noted in the second subject of the first movement, the symbol for these accents is >. This fact, considered in connection with the other relevant data referred to, establishes beyond doubt that the accents in this symphony so symbolized are eminently melodic and expressive, and not percussive or dynamic. These two fall on notes which would naturally be the most expressive ones, considering the melodic and harmonic data; and the composer obviously wished to make as sure as possible that the desired intensification would materialize in performance. Above all details stands the philosophical mood of this movement, on its sublime plane of the love and peace that pass all understanding. Every detail in it must contribute to that over-all impression and not attract the hearer's attention to itself. The accents here, then, should be type 22, or better yet, if they can be realized, 33.

The other pair of bars containing accents is that which follows both of the bars in which the trumpets enter. *(Fig. 25)* In each instance the dynamics, beginning a bar previously with the trumpet entrance, are *forte;* the accents are on each of the first two dotted quarters of the bar, and on the third dotted quarter the dynamics become *fortissimo.* Both of these outbursts, if considered strictly by themselves, without relation to their place in the movement as a whole, might be viewed as rather military in character; but when seen in their fuller significance they are understood to be declamatory and nobly solemn, particularly as they serve to illuminate important cadential points in the movement's structure. These accents, therefore, should not be acute either. Nor should they include the lengthening factor, for the accented notes are also dotted, as were the last accents to be discussed in the first movement, and they are also followed by rests (but at the same time one should be sure not to shorten them). This leaves the factors of color and volume, and they are both appropriate here. But the accented notes, being *forte,* would consequently sound *fortissimo;* would this not improperly anticipate the *fortissimo* which follows?

The great virtue of accents is that they affect only the one designated note, while dynamic levels hold good for the entire passage until the next dynamic indication. Therefore when the *fortissimo* enters, it applies to the sixteenth-notes between the eighths on the main beats, as well as to the eighths; but before that, the accents apply only to the eighth-notes, leaving the sixteenths entirely untouched. Accordingly there is a clear distinction between the two levels, and the written *fortissimo* is not improperly anticipated; so type 25 is seen to be right.

The accents in the vocal parts of the *finale* do not properly belong in a survey of this kind and will not again be referred to here. It is only pointed out that due notice should be taken of them according to the principles described herein, the meaning of the text, and the conditions of vocal production. However, in the orchestral parts there are some accents to which attention should be called. One of them occurs in the first statement of the main theme by the full orchestra. *(Fig. 26)* The accents occur only in the wind parts (not the strings or percussion, nor the contra-bassoon, which Beethoven ordinarily treats as just a reinforcement of the double-basses) on the first note of the repetition of the first four-bar phrase, and on the first note of the repetition of the eight-bar phrase. The dynamics are *forte,* the tempo, *allegro,* the symbol *sf;* this is the fourth and last repetition of the entire theme in this section— the first having been on the celli and basses unaccompanied, and each subsequent one with larger and louder orchestration and fuller harmonization. This last announcement, then, is in the nature of a climax, a joyous one too; the whole orchestra has enthusiastically taken up the new song, soon to be supplemented by the human voices. The music here, while still on the sublime plane of the symphony as a whole, is energetic and triumphant, not introspective; therefore an acute accent is called for. And since the accents occur only on the repetitions, they are not thematic, but purely emphatic; accordingly an intensifying color should also be included, but not a volume factor (unless required for proper balance). What, if any, deduction can be drawn from the fact that the strings and percussion are entirely unaccented? (For they do not join in the melody, but play only harmony, and in short detached notes, oddly enough, in the style of classical brass parts, while here Beethoven has the brass behaving like strings!) The fact can but confirm our conclusion that the accents were intended solely to intensify the beginnings of the repetitions of the phrases of the theme, and not to produce loud crashes. So we have the factors of acuteness and color on the first of the accents—type 13—and on the second, which is not slurred to its succeeding note, it would be well also to include the lengthening factor, making the type 14.

The next accents—on the beginning of each of the two bars immediately preceding the *"poco ritenente"*—find the dynamics, tempo and orchestration the same as at the previous accent. *(Fig. 27)* Here the accent in each bar is on the tonic of the dominant key, attained here at last after a considerable passage of restless harmony, whetting the hearer's desire for a resting place. And it is that welcome resting place —a half-note, a unison A, that is accented, in both bars, though it is played by different choirs in each of the two bars, while the other choirs have an unaccented running figure. The instruments that play that A fill out their bars with two quarter-note E's marked with *staccato* dots. The musical feeling of the passage calls for a "sitting down" on the A's and a lightening of the tone on the E's; and it is precisely this impression that Beethoven is confirming by accenting the A's and marking the E's *staccato*. The accent type needed to satisfy the requirements of the situation is no less than 17—and it will also be well to play the E's in these bars somewhat less heavily than normal in order to bring out the full strength of the accented A's.

The next accents occur immediately after the first exit of the voices in the Alla Marcia section. The orchestra continues with a double fugue, in a continuous *fortissimo*. *(Fig. 28)* The time signature is six-eight, the tempo *vivace;* and the rhythm of the first two bars of one of the subjects is an eighth-note on the third eighth of the bar followed by a dotted quarter-note on the fourth eighth. The dotted quarter is marked *sf;* and in the string parts it is always tied over to a quarter-note on the same pitch in the next bar. The wind parts that participate in this subject have the same pattern as the strings, with this one difference: their dotted quarters are not prolonged into the following bar. The reason for this difference is obscure; one can only surmise that Beethoven felt it as hopeless in his day to expect a wind player to hold his tone over a bar-line as we do in ours.

Be that as it may, the simultaneous differing patterns of the choirs on the same thematic material pose a rare and knotty question. In support of a judgment that the accent must include the lengthening factor, one could point out that the prolonged tone in the strings becomes dissonant as it crosses the bar-line, twice in succession, and that in both bars the next note is consonant, being a stepwise resolution upward of the prolonged tone in both cases (technically a "retardation" rather than a "resolution," but let us stick to the general and less technical term). In such cases it is natural and proper to keep the dissonant tone viable as far as its resolution. Letting it die before it resolves makes the resolution sound like a fresh start—and that would contradict the musical grammar of the passage, for a resolution is not a beginning but a termination.

On the negative side, one could point out that had Beethoven wished the accented tone to sound in its full strength up to the point of resolution, he certainly would have kept it sustained in the winds as well as the strings; and that he must have deliberately cut the winds off at the bar-line for the express purpose of making the resolution sound not like a resolution but like a fresh start. In view of the contradictory considerations, perhaps the best one can do with the situation is to take "fielder's choice."

As to the remaining factors, let us observe that this section is unquestionably military in character, and hence a "bite" is in order. As for color and volume, the following points are to be considered: in all marches, including this one, the beats that fall on the beginning of each bar are the strongest ones. In this march this difference is a slight one, inasmuch as throughout most of its course the bar-line beat in the principal voice falls on a tone held over from the previous bar, where it originated on the light beat with an accent. If the accents are made too large, the proper pulsation of the march will be overbalanced. Therefore the accents will be best effectuated by imparting to the accented tones an extra vital color throughout their duration, and by attacking them with a "bite." Thus the type is 13; and as another important element in the accents, the eighth-note preceding each one should be played slightly more lightly than normal. But care must be taken that these eighth-notes will not come late, since they are at the same time resolutions of their predecessors and anticipations of their successors. The playing of two adjacent notes in different colors, characters, and/or dynamic levels, while still placing each note precisely on its correct rhythmic instant, calls for more effort and mastery than most orchestral musicians, even the best ones, normally can or care to exhibit.

In this symphony only one more accent needs to be noted; that is the one following the first appearance of the words "seid umschlungen Millionen." *(Fig. 29)* This phrase is in its conception one of the most spacious and noble in the whole work: it is too often spoiled in performance by the well-meaning but catastrophic attempts of the male contingent of most choruses to negotiate with conviction that brave leap of a major ninth up to E. And those worthy gentlemen who succeed in making it are so proud of their achievement that they shout the E with a stridency that effectually destroys whatever atmosphere of solemnity may still remain. However, such happenings must not discourage the quest for beauty. Let us take a closer look at the music. The dynamics are *fortissimo,* the tempo a slow three-halves, with no notes shorter than halves. The orchestration consists only of celli, basses, and one trombone. The phrase is a floating, rhythmless unison strongly suggestive of plain-chant. An acute attack on the accented tone would be out of character. The lengthening factor is not applicable either. Color? Yes, a noble tone. Volume? Probably not, except optionally for some extra pressure at the very inception of the tone; the dynamics being already *ff,* the prospect of a note sustained *fff* for a whole long bar's duration is decidedly unattractive. Therefore we have here an accent of type 22 or 25; also in the second bar following, at the word "der," which is *not* accented in the vocal parts, further indicating that the accents in the orchestra should not be too conspicuous. It will be seen that similar considerations apply to all the accents in this section.

Mention must be made of one example, at any rate, from Beethoven's orchestral creation, which clearly demonstrates not only the necessity, but also Beethoven's keen awareness, of class C accents. It occurs in the seventh bar of the *Violin Concerto,* and the same bar of the theme where it is later joined by the solo violin. *(Fig. 30)* The accent, here indicated by *sf,* is on a dotted half-note preceded by a *crescendo* and followed by a *diminuendo.* The chord is a ninth (notwithstanding the omission of the third and fifth) and it constitutes the peak of the eight-bar period; the orchestration comprises woodwinds only. From its first appearance, it is clear that the accent must include the volume factor, and that it is a plain one, as all the voices of it are slurred to the preceding note in each voice—in fact, the bassoons sustain the same note. The lengthening factor is not involved, since the accented tone is quitted as well as begun with slurs in all voices. Color, too, is called for, since, as mentioned, the accented note is the peak of the phrase. This analysis covers all the questions that can arise except this: at what point of the tone's duration should the accent's effectuation be the greatest?

From the appearance of this seventh bar, one could very well decide that it should be at the tone's inception. But before we can be sure of this, we must realize that even when a composer means an accent to be effectuated mainly at some other point, he has no means of indicating it in writing; for according to our musical notation, a sustained tone is written as just one note, of its full value, not split up into a chain of notes of lesser value,* all capable of being differently marked; nor, on such a single long note, can the accent symbol be written at any place other than directly above or below the note—and thus it must always look as if the accent is to be imparted at the tone's inception †—even though

---

* There are two exceptions to this statement, neither of which is involved here: (1) where, notably in operatic orchestrations, one often finds such figures as a quarter note tied to an eighth of the same pitch following it, which could be written equally well, strictly speaking, as a dotted quarter, but which is written that way to emphasize that the tone should be sustained; and (2) where there is no single note, however dotted, available to indicate the exact length of time a given tone is to be sustained.

† As we have noted in chapter 2, with reference to Cannabich.

crescendo-diminuendo marks on single tones are quite common (too common, perhaps?). At any rate, one must always bear in mind that it is perfectly possible that an accent whose symbol appears simultaneously with its note's beginning may be intended to sound somewhere else along the line—anywhere else, before the tone is finished.

To make ourselves sure about this one, let us look at the spot where the same theme is joined by the solo violin. The orchestral material is identical with that at the beginning, accent and all. The solo violin sings the same theme, with the addition of some connective and decorative notes, an octave above the highest instrument of the orchestra. On the beat on which the orchestra's accented note begins, the solo violin has a passing tone, unaccented, of a quarter-note, reaching the octave of the orchestra's melody note on the SECOND quarter; and it is *this* note, the *second* quarter, in the solo violin part which is accented!

It should be too obvious for further comment that because of this the orchestra's accent also actually takes place on the second quarter. And it seems natural that this will also apply to the introductory statement of the same theme by the orchestra alone. Thus we have at least one unmistakable example in Beethoven of a class C accent—type 36.

Thus we take leave of Beethoven, the mighty; who notwithstanding his relentless poundings of musical materials into forms that could convey what he had to say, remains first, last, and throughout, a supreme and consummate artist.

FIVE

SCHUBERT

No better source of examples for this study could be found than Schubert's *Seventh Symphony in C Major*. This glorious work, in which are blended so many elements of both epic and lyrical materials, is liberally sprinkled with accents on whose interpretation the proper projection of the work largely depends.

At the very outset we are confronted with a series of accents on the first note of each bar of the opening theme, in both its initial statement in the horns alone, and its counterstatement in the woodwinds. Its literal performance would bring about an emphasis (the type of which does not presently matter) on each bar-line which would effectively destroy the melodic flow of the theme; and we know from its later transformations, as well as from the composer's general style, that this would be utterly contrary to his conception. The theme is of eight bars;

but it is made up, not of two four-bar phrases, but of two phrases of three bars each and a two-bar augmentation of the sixth bar. This phrase structure also would be thwarted by a literal performance of the accents. One must, therefore, bring to bear on the problem all the resources—technical, critical, and poetic—that one can muster. *(Fig. 31)*

Commencing a symphony with an unaccompanied horn theme is an eminently "romantic" procedure; one must look, then, to the personal and emotional values. If the dynamics here were *forte,* one might be justified in analogizing this situation to that of Schumann's *Spring* Symphony, and conclude that this is like a proud summons to Spring, of which every note should be bravely and equally blared forth; but here the dynamics are *piano,* and besides, the contour of the theme is more flowing than a real flourish would be. To disregard the accents entirely, on the other hand, would be to introduce this great symphony with a diffident voice from another world, as in the overture to *Oberon* —an interpretation which is additionally refuted by the differing characters of the music following the horn openings, by the range of this majestic work, and by the fact that here the scoring is for *two* horns in unison, with which the *Oberon* effect is virtually impossible to obtain.

Having eliminated all possible interpretations but one, the deduction remains that the accents are shorthand directions for the character of the performance of the theme as a whole: *viz.,* calm, yet with sustained vitality in the tone and a slightly more vigorous attack of each note than would be used in a typical unaccented horn melody. The accents should be thought of as one on every note, and of type 23 (with still a slight separation between the notes); except that (1) the last two bars, being *pp* and unaccented, should have no accents, and (2) the first note of the fourth bar should have a type 26 accent, as it begins an intensified repetition of the opening phrase (as this is the highest note in the whole theme, the players ordinarily give it a slight additional dynamic force anyway because of the greater tension required in producing the tone on their instruments).

When the woodwinds take up the counterstatement, the absence of accent on their first note signifies that their entrance should not be an actual "effect," but that their entrance should seem merely to continue

the quiet line begun by the strings in their bridge figure of the preceding bar; and their accents in the *following* bars indicate a gradual
assertion of their own characteristic styles and timbres.

The remainder of the introduction and the first subject of the *allegro*
call for no particular comment here. One of Schubert's typical abrupt
modulations, made with one dramatic and simple stroke, prepares the
second subject. The score of this musical idea (fifth bar after letter D
in the Breitkopf & Härtel edition), at first glance, suggests a light dance
movement; but on further examination it becomes evident that that
cannot be its intended character, for not only would it, in that case, not
contrast sufficiently with the preceding rhythmical material, but also its
continuation, cast as it is in the mood of faery melancholy which is
peculiarly Schubert's, could not be forced into such a conception. *(Fig.
32)* This interpretation is further confirmed by the presence of mur-
muring figures in the strings, sustained tones in the brass, and also by
an accent (!) on the *second* half of the third and fourth bars. Thus one
sees that while usually it requires musical analysis to clarify the meaning of accents, it is also possible for the presence of an accent to contribute to the musical analysis. Here it does so by pointing out that after
two virtually identical bars, which, according to the pattern of so
many themes, merely "mark time," the theme sets out from home base
in a direction and leads through a mysterious triplet up to a resting
place on the weak beat of the third bar. The composer could not have
indicated more plainly than he did that the rhythm of the third bar is
just the opposite of that of the first two: that the melodic curve is not
"anchored" anywhere between the first beat of the second bar and the
second beat of the third bar, and all the intervening tones must be "slid
over" so as to keep the melody constantly in suspension and moving
toward its objective of the next "anchoring" point (without, of course,
hurrying the tempo). It is thus especially important to avoid an accent
on the first beat of the third bar—in fact, it will be helpful to play that
spot with the opposite of an accent, a deliberate lightening. The theme
played correctly in this manner, with this unexpected but inevitable
displacement of accent, admits of no superficial terpsichorean associa-
tions, and shows itself to be predominantly lyrical and pathetic, and
rhythmical only in its mechanics. Knowing this, we now have the key

to the first two bars: the *staccato* dots indicate that the notes should be well separated, while our analysis shows that they should not be so short as to be dry; the accents are of type 6 or 7. And the accent in the third bar should be type 26; purely expressive, not at all percussive. To overlook such small but pregnant details would result in a failure, in great part, to realize in performance such a subtle and personal genius as Schubert's.

At the first *forte* after the entrance of the second subject (letter E in the Breitkopf & Härtel score) more accents appear. *(Fig. 33)* The basses have one on the first note of a three-note figure, a form of the initial three-note motive of the second subject. And while here it is *forte,* though at its first appearance it was *piano,* the accent type is the same, except for the consideration that the music here is no longer gently plaintive, but dramatic and energetic. Therefore an acute attack is called for, making the type 3 or 4. The remainder of the orchestra (except for the drums) has a figure which is new here: a quarter-note upbeat, *staccato* and *forte,* and a dotted half-note on an unexpected chord, followed by moving notes in *piano* beginning on the fourth quarter, in the nature of a relaxing contrast, or an answering murmur. Now in some parts—violins, violas, trumpets, and trombones—these dotted half-notes are marked *ff* and not accented. All the remaining parts are accented *(fz)* without a dynamic direction except for the *f* on the preceding note, the upbeat. The plan in all this is seen to be as follows: the composer has carefully avoided giving accents to the instruments most likely to be overassertive, while he has accented those which are certain to be unobtrusive but which will yet serve to impart the initial "bite." The total effect he was aiming at was an accent, in *fortissimo,* without stridency; and it is achieved by the exact means that he prescribed, provided the written accents are correctly diagnosed and effectuated, and accents are carefully avoided in the nonaccented parts. While the *fortissimo* in the latter should not be read into the accented parts, it throws light on the type of accent to be applied in them; and this, we conclude, is not only acute, but also with the volume factor at the tone's inception, in order to hold their own with their powerful comrades; and, to achieve a resplendent tone quality, here called for by the harmony, the color factor should be included. One can perceive a further purpose in this "mixed" marking: to make the accented note, while more vigorous than its predecessor, not so much so as to rupture the melodic line; for this point is only one of the several peaks in the "ridge" which had begun with the second subject—it is not a dramatic intrusion on it, and must not sound as if it were.

As to the accent's duration, if the note is sustained to its full value, the brief *piano* contrast which follows immediately will not be fully realized, because of both the resonance of the accented chord and the practical impossibility of making such an abrupt change from *ff* to *p* in purely instrumental technique; therefore the note must be slightly shortened, and an open breathing space left slightly before the end of its written value is reached; so, the accent type is 18, the only example of this rare type encountered so far.

Now a word concerning the symbols. Up to this point in this work, all the accents have been symbolized by >. At letter E, for the first time in this symphony, we meet the typically "romantic" hybrid *fz*. However, the difference in symbol, as was the case with Haydn, is utterly of no account; for at the same point of the recapitulation (letter K) as letter E is of the exposition, the whole orchestra has the symbol >. Writing at white heat as he did, Schubert must have assumed that what he had made clear in one passage would remain clear at the passage's reappearance.

That passage is followed by two six-bar phrases, the second of which is essentially a repetition of the first. In both, the first and third bars are filled by an augmented sixth chord which resolves to a triad that fills the second bar and half of the fourth. The dynamics at the beginning of the first six-bar phrase are *ff* in all parts; and there is no further mark in the first phrase except a *fz* in the bass parts (including celli and trombones; every note is a whole note) in the third bar. These *fz*'s will be referred to as accent A. *(Fig. 34)* Now in these first four bars of both six-bar phrases, this augmented-sixth-resolution progression occurs twice, each time extending over two bars. In the regular course of musical performance, the transition from discord to resolution would be inflected with some kind of relaxation or lessening of tension, commencing before the point of resolution, and continuing after. There is no reason to make an exception here; in fact, there is a good reason, namely the accent, to include this passage in the general principle. It indicates, among other things, that after the relaxing resolution in the second bar of the discord of the first, the next discord that resolves (which is marked accent A) must be stressed with renewed force. But in the third bar, does the composer want a force exactly equal to that of the first, or greater? It seems that if he had wanted only equal force, he could safely have entrusted his wishes to any competent performers without further ado; as he did not do this, but marked an accent on the second discord, he seems to have wanted a greater stress there, thus making the second pair of bars more emphatic than the first. If we denote relative degrees of force, stress, or intensity by numbers, with 1 denoting the greatest, then the pattern of the first three bars of this phrase is, 2-3-1—that is, the third bar has the greatest stress, the first the next greatest, and the second bar the least. The type of accent, as it must have existed in Schubert's mind, will be discussed below after we have had a look at what happens in the second six bars, in which the first six bars are repeated with some modifications.

In the second six bars, the bass consists not of whole-notes but of quarter-notes, grouped in threes so as to indicate the three-note motive previously mentioned, this time the interval between the first two quarter-notes being an octave; the brass also cease to have whole-notes but have instead dotted halves, their last quarter consisting of an upbeat on which they join the woodwinds, which alone had the upbeat in the first phrase; and the trumpets, in place of their previous whole-notes, now play only half-notes on the *second* half of each bar. The total effect is to add more movement and significance to the second, third, and fourth quarters of each bar, thus adding vitality to the musical feeling as a whole. The first quarter, however, is not added to—surely the addition of the flutes and oboes with the loss of the trumpets is not a net gain—therefore, so as to support this increased vitality, and also to enable the first beat of every bar to still retain its same relative force, one would expect all the first beats to have accents; and this is exactly what we find.

The first beats of each of the first three bars of the second six-bar phrase bear the symbol *fz*. Let us call these accents B, C, and D respectively. Obviously they indicate an emphasis superior to anything in the preceding phrase, for they occur in every voice (except the trumpets, which do not enter till the third quarter); and as the dynamics have not been modified since the previous mark of *ff*, what we have now is all of that plus something more. Now what is this something more?

To begin with, as to the duration factor, there are notes of four different values bearing the accent simultaneously: sixteenth (timpani), eighth (violins), quarter (basses), and dotted half (remainder). Which of them determines the accent's duration? Let us consider first the three-note motive in the basses (and celli). If the second and third notes were accented equally with the first, the accent on the first, which is thematic as well as expressive, would not stand out accordingly; therefore in this voice the accent must be no longer than the first quarter note. And while the motive is not marked with *staccato* dots, as it was in its previous appearances, it still should not be played sustained, even though with separate bows; for if it were, it would lose its character and structural significance; therefore all three notes should be played for the full normal length of quarter notes, that is, slightly separated. As to the type of accent to be given to the first of them, the energetic character of the passage calls for an acute attack; and the element of its emphasis by means of repetition with accents calls for expressive color. Considering the rapid tempo, and the consequent shortness of time for the accent to assert itself, a volume factor would also be helpful. Therefore the type of accent to be imparted would be 16; and its duration should be co-extensive with its tone's. So much for the basses. As to the rest of the orchestra, the question arises whether this is an instance of two or more simultaneous musical "molecules," or of but one consisting of the combination of all the different things that are going on. Notwithstanding a technically arguable case for the former, the preponderance of rational and musical analysis favors the latter—for the whole harmonic progression, with its rhythmical activity, leading as it does into the first large cadence of the second subject, is far more organic and essential here than any one or more of its parts. Hence, the accents in all parts should be of the same duration; and the bass, being the only part having thematic significance, must be the guide of the duration. Accordingly the dotted halves are accented for only their first half's (one quarter-note) duration. The violins, with their perpetual detached eighth-note motion, will also have the same type accent on their first two eighth-notes of each bar. Not only does this solution conform musically to the foregoing considerations, but also, with regard to the violinistic idiom and the part of the violins here, it enables the violins to continue playing with the same part of their bows—as it calls for an upstroke equal to the downstroke—and it assists the harmony to be brought out, with its emphasis on the second note as well as the first. In the timpani, the roll in sixteenth-notes, at an accented *ff,* which the score prescribes, is a practical impossibility; there is no question of striking the drum eight times in the first half-bar at any tempo at which this music could reasonably move. The conductor should decide whether he wants four or six strokes—both are equally within the range of Schubert's indications—and have those constituting the first quarter's value struck more sharply than the following ones. So much for the duration of the accent; we have not yet determined whether the accent will cause a prolongation of the trailing portion of the long tones. It seems here that it certainly should, and for this reason: in the first six-bar phrase, the notes corresponding to those accented here, are (except in the violins and woodwinds) all whole-notes, and if the notes in the second phrase—which we have found to be an emphatic repetition—are not prolonged beyond their normal duration, they will sound less emphatic than they did in the first phrase; and of course they, as well as everything else possible, must sound more emphatic in the second phrase.

The entire foregoing paragraph applies to the accents B, C, and D. To this extent they are alike, but in other respects now to be discussed they differ. In the first six-bar phrase we saw how the stress pattern of the first three bars was capable of being represented by the numbers 2-3-1. Now should this stress pattern be impressed on the second phrase, being, as it is, a virtual repetition of the first? Undoubtedly yes; the repetition ought to have everything that the first statement had, and more if possible. So finally we are in a position to choose the types of accent in each voice of accents B, C, and D. As already discussed, the basses have type 16 in all. The woodwinds, horns, trombones, and violas should have 11 at B, 20 at C, and 17 at D; and the violins, 10 at B, 19 at C, and 16 at D.

Now let us return to accent A, and we shall have done with this intricate problem. The type of accent will be determined by considering the foregoing discussion together with the fact that accent A appears only in the bass voice. The factors desired here are, first, lengthening; for the accented tone, which is a whole note, resolves by a descent of one half step, and the resolution will be more musically correct if well connected. Color, too, is necessary, for the accentuation is in the interest of intensity; and the color should be sustained as long as the tone. As to the other factors, let us be aware that this accent must be of a less large quantity than its counterpart in the second or repeated phrase, accent D, for everything in the second phrase must be larger or more intense than its counterpart in the first, wherever possible. As to the acuteness and volume factors, if accent A were to have them both, the following consequences would ensue: the accented tones would partially cover the unaccented simultaneous ones, the total sound would come very close to equaling that of accent D, and a volume louder than *ff* sustained throughout most or all of a bar in the trombones would be both ugly and out of the spirit of the music. But an acute attack without the volume factor would well effectuate the accent and be fully consistent with the musical character. Furthermore, that seems to be what Schubert "heard" here; for while in the true bass instruments, the accented note is below its predecessor, the second and third trombones, which play in unison with the bass and are also accented, leap upward to their accented note from its predecessor! And this notwithstanding that they could perfectly well, within their normal range, have descended along with the other instruments with which they are in unison. An acute attack is a normal incident of such a movement on a trombone, particularly in a passage already marked *ff*. Therefore the accent type called for here is 14.

At the end of the second of these six-bar phrases, the long-postponed cadence is finally achieved; and with it the principal second subject reappears, in its new-found major key; but its accents have now been displaced from the first quarter of each bar to the fourth, and each bar's accent is larger than that of the preceding bar (as Schubert was at pains to indicate). In fact, the third bar's is so large, particularly in the duration factor, that it is marked as being slurred into its succeeding note. Observe the unexpected-inevitable modification Schubert made in his theme, purely by the shift of the accent the distance of one note; this is but one inconspicuous example of his boundless charm and resource. The accent types here are, obviously, 23, 26, and 16 respectively —and they are the same in the repetition of the four-bar phrase which immediately follows.

But the exposition is not yet over; Schubert must have a further word, here consisting of a development of a motive from the theme of the introduction, in the trombones. *(Fig. 35)* It is garlanded about with much activity in the remainder of the orchestra, among which accented sustained tones in the celli and woodwinds recur regularly. The conductor should choose his accents from the following types, some of which now appear in this study for the first time: 8, 14, 20, 23, 28, 34. No further discussion should be needed as a guide to the remaining accents in the first movement.

The second movement—perhaps the fastest "slow" movement in all the great symphonic literature—opens with a melody in the bass, which never reappears. *(Fig. 36)* In the seven-bar course of this melody, only five quarter-notes occur, all the others being shorter; every one of the shorter notes bears a *staccato* dot, and every one of the quarter-notes bears an accent. This fact confirms what one can sense from the nature of the melody itself, that the quarter-notes must be enriched somehow, and the others touched quite lightly. Type 23 on all the accented notes should best subserve the musical idea here. The imaginative interpreter could well feel a perceptible *crescendo* from the third bar through the fifth, each one beginning with its searching E approached each time by more elaborate and insistent steps; and then a relapse to the original ground level. In such a case the amount of each accent will, of course, vary with the exact dynamic plane at that point.

The great melody which then enters in the oboe deserves special attention not only for its key role in the movement's structure, but also for its abundance of accents. Its first bar is the same as the fourth bar of the introductory bass melody of the movement—a detail often unnoticed—with the difference that the accent is omitted and a passing grace note inserted (this difference is among those mighty trifles which demonstrate more than fastidious taste, even more than a profound and intimate grasp of instrumental characters—they truly reach toward the transcendent and inscrutable essence of Music itself). In the order in which the accents appear in the melody, they should have the following types: 23, 22, 25 or 36, 22, 6, 6, 33, 33. The reasons are these: this being a gentle, plaintive strain in a dynamic plane no higher than *piano,* acute attacks and dynamic accents would not normally be appropriate. Now, considering the third bar, with its two E's, let us recall the general principle that repeated notes should be varied in their inflection. Here the second E is less intense or weighted than the first; therefore its accent should be a lighter one. As was pointed out regarding the introductory bass melody, to which the oboe melody is related, the accents clearly indicate a lengthening factor; and the only additional available accenting factor is that of color. Thus type 23 is called for. But the second E not only is lighter, but also rounds off the first phrase of the melody and should provide some slight breathing space before the start of the second phrase; for this combination of reasons, then, the second E's accent should be different from the first E's by the omission of the lengthening factor.

The second phrase begins at the fourth bar, and its first note is an accented quarter. The chord is a diminished seventh—one of considerable restlessness. For both these reasons, this accent should be the most emphatic one so far; and to make it so, let us add a volume factor to those present in the first accent of the preceding bar. There are three types of accent with which this can be done: 25, 36, or a class E accent in which expressive color is present at the inception of the tone and the volume factor added in the form of a *crescendo,* followed by a *diminuendo.* The last mentioned would be the most exquisite.

The conclusions here reached as to both the gentleness and the superiority of this accent are substantiated by a glance at the entire score at this point, where we find that the violins and violas continue on their imperturbable way without accent, but the basses are given the first accent they have had since the oboe entrance. In other words, this is the peak of the music so far, but not such a prominent or emphatic peak as to enlist the violins and violas to its combined forces. The basses' accent, of course, should also be gentle—say type 22. The fifth bar of the oboe solo, containing the second accent of the second phrase, begins with a resolution of the preceding bar's discord. As we have remarked previously, such a point calls for a lessening of stress; therefore, although the accent is marked precisely like the preceding one, the color factor alone must suffice for this one. No duration factor can be involved here, as the accented note is slurred to its successor. Now we are up to the accented B's in the next two bars, which are the last notes whose accents we have already designated. Probably the best way of effectuating these accents, which surely are purely expressive ones, within the *diminuendo* indicated in the score, is by the suggested choice of types, becoming gradually less perceptible.

After one repetition of the melody, in which the clarinet doubles the oboe, the mode changes to major. The first note of the second and fifth bars of the major strain is accented; but as this is only to clarify the change to major, it should take no accent other than type 22. This type, and, where applicable, type 23 also, will be found to be those most frequently used throughout this movement. The most notable instances are the accents in the four bars preceding the first appearance of the F major second subject, and those in the horns in the unforgettable and much-celebrated passage just before the recapitulation; although in the latter passage, types 26 and 37 are also artistically justifiable. *(Fig. 37)*

Detailed discussion of the accents in the remainder of this movement should now be superfluous. A few noteworthy instances, however, may be pointed out. Firstly, in the section between the dramatic climax of the movement, and the return of the second subject (after letter I), the *absence* of accents in the cello and oboe cantilenas, amid a great surrounding profusion of accents, demands the most tranquil, sustained, and singing manner of delivery that is possible, with only the smoothest and most gradual of nuances. *(Fig. 38)* Secondly, the accent in the fourth bar after letter L (the twenty-sixth bar preceding the end of the movement) will be best effectuated by type 33. It is on a minor subdominant "resolution" of an orthodox dominant seventh; both chords occupy a whole bar, are in *piano* and accented and are scored for woodwinds, with the strings punctuating both with the same chords *pizzicato* on the second beat of both bars. *(Fig. 39)* This harmonic "resolution" has not occurred before, and its effect is of an abrupt hush, or deadening of color. The whole coda, in fact, abounds in dramatic effects. The thematic material of the movement breaks up into dreary scraps, gathers itself together in defiant cries, and again collapses; the major mode is conspicuous by its absence. For consistency's sake this chord of dark evasion should have a dark and dead sound, in contrast with the expectant nature of its predecessor; moreover, the dramatic effect will be heightened by a slight *luftpause* between the two. And in the second bar it will be better to slightly delay the strings' *pizzicato,* than to have it too soon, and better to have it too dry than too vibrant.

Finally, the last eleven bars are wonderfully instructive. *(Fig. 40)* Let us observe the ultimate development of the "germ" of the two repeated notes of the original oboe theme. Here, in the bars in which they are marked less than *forte,* only the first of the two notes is accented—this fact confirms our analysis of the second being lighter than the first; but when they occur in *fortissimo,* both notes are accented! How dire and terrible those two innocent E's have become! And how still more dire and terrible are the two firmament-defying F's! After this, not even Schubert can attempt to express more. If ever a scherzo were needed for blowing away an unbearably beautiful and overpowering sadness, it is here.

As far as accents are concerned, the scherzo presents no new problems—though it affords many examples of the rare types 1, 2, and 3. And in the cosmic *finale,* the first four accents seem to be for the purpose of vitalizing and sustaining the tone *(Fig. 41)*—their type, therefore, should be 14, as should all those, in both the winds and strings, in such passages as that immediately following letter I. But most of the accents in the movement, other than those on half notes, lack the lengthening factor—for if they were to include it, the rhythmic whirl would tend to bog down. For the four repeated notes of the main second subject, a "floating" character is indicated by the slurs and dots with which they are marked—that is, all the tones equal, with a calm, sustained, level feeling, and without agitation, determination, or the impression of setting foot down anywhere. *(Fig. 42)* How are we to synthesize this character with the accents? A study of the score a little farther on will help to answer this question. At the closing cadence of the first statement of the theme, we find the four notes marked the same way as before, except that the accents are now absent. And as before, the dynamics are *piano*. But now, without the slightest attempt at transition, the theme recommences in a new key with much reduced orchestration, in *pianissimo,* and with an accent on each note!

So now we know, at least, that the accent lacks the volume factor; for common sense tells us that a composer would not mark two adjacent notes differently if he intended them to sound alike. That is to say, if the accent included a volume factor, the *pianissimo* with accent would be identical with the *piano* without accent; and to thus reason would make futile all attempts to produce differences in inflection of tone. But it is clear that the accent has expressive purpose; for the cadence, from which it is absent, is a point of repose, of stability, of completion; and with the unexpected chord (major mediant) that begins the restatement of the theme, the point instantly becomes one of activity and expectancy. The renewed activity, then, should be reflected in the tone quality, and thus we know that the accent must have a color factor. It also seems beyond contradiction that it must have a lengthening factor; for the slurs extend over four bars, and these slurs, if they are not to be entirely ignored, must be so taken into consideration along with the accent symbols.

There remains one factor to be considered—is the accent acute? On this factor interpretation can reasonably differ, depending on whether the conductor's conception is prevailingly rhythmical or lyrical; both are admissible. If it is decided to have the accent acute, the type is 14; if plain, then type 23 or 25 (the volume factor being present only at the tone's inception). Some conductors feel a *diminuendo* on each note also; however, this is highly questionable, as for quite a long stretch the dynamic level is *pp*.

Let us return to consider one accent often overlooked—that on the dotted quarter in the sixth bar of the second subject. *(Fig. 42)* Although a class A accent is conceivable on it, a class B one would be more appropriate—type 22, or, to be more assertive about it, 19.

It should be observed that in the first sixteen bars of the theme, all the winds have accents on all their repeated notes; but later, when the trumpets and third trombone enter, the woodwinds which have been accented all along continue so, but the brass that enters is unmarked except for the dynamics. Such, again, are Schubert's mighty subtleties.

SIX

MENDELSSOHN

One might well expect Mendelssohn, the most impeccable of the great Romantics, to have formulated a consistent and manifest system of accentuation. Let us scrutinize two of his finest and best loved orchestral works—one from his youth (so far as he ever had any, musically speaking), the other from his early but consummate maturity—the *Hebrides Overture,* and the *Italian Symphony.* Throughout them he uses the two most usual symbols for his accents, and both about equally often. But when one makes an attempt to decipher his rationale, one finds each symbol used in contrasting contexts, and the two different symbols used in identical contexts, not only between the two works named, but also within the same work. Additional works of his serve only to furnish further illustrations of this finding. Therefore it can be asserted irrefutably that in interpreting the accents in Mendelssohn's works, one cannot be guided in the slightest degree by the symbol he chose.

This does not mean that the two symbols were identical in Mendelssohn's thinking. In reading his scores one can acquire a feeling of his conception of them, on noticing, for example, that while he puts > on every one of a rapid succession of eighth-notes, he never puts sf's so close together. Although he uses both symbols in equal abundance, he evidently had a vague notion, speciously imbibed along with his excellent classical discipline, that a sf might imply something more exalted than the relatively "lowly" >, even though the two might sound precisely alike! And so, at that, in his scrupulous pseudo-traditional taste, if not in his clarity, he did adhere to a certain limited and utterly useless consistency. For example, in the relatively few cases where he uses different symbols to mark accents within any one phrase, or in different appearances of the same phrase, and the accents are of unequal amplitude, it is always the larger accent that bears the sf (the larger accent being made so, of course, only by the context). Doubtless he intended us to make use of his accent marks as assistance in interpreting his music; but the truth is that our analysis goes in just the opposite direction.

Numberless examples could be cited to show Mendelssohn's real lack of system in his choice of symbols. One in which it appears most clearly is the passage leading to the first appearance of the second subject in the scherzo from the *Midsummer Night's Dream* music—the passage begins with the first sf in the piece. *(Fig. 43)* Observe the sf's and >'s scattered indiscriminately on similar notes. Incidentally, the vitality of those notes in the woodwinds and first violins marked sf must be sustained into their successors—the duration factor is the cardinal one with them. The whole point of them is that the first and second time they resolve similarly, upwards, but the third time they fool us and resolve downwards. Nobody need worry about the resolving tones, the accented ones, being conspicuous to the players and hearers; but the players must be made well aware of the significance of the short tones to which they resolve, so that the hearers will not miss this delightful point.

While we are discussing this piece, let us digress just a moment to study one particular accent in it—*viz.,* the only one (except for its repetition) in the second subject. *(Fig. 44)* Every time this theme comes around, this same note bears the only accent, and always with the symbol >. The note is a quarter, and is the only note in the whole theme that is either not *staccato* or longer than an eighth-note, and it is both. The dynamics are *piano* or *pianissimo,* and the tempo is quite fast, one beat in each ⅜ bar. The accented note is the seventh in the chord of the dominant seventh—the only time, too, that this chord occurs in the course of the theme, and the bar contains no different chord. The uniqueness of this combination of long tone and unusual chord produces a feeling of "sitting down"—and this feeling is heightened by the accent, and evidently is the reason for it. The type should be 23, according to these considerations: the music trips daintily along, wonderfully suggesting the fairies in Shakespeare's play. An acute attack and a volume factor would defeat that achievement, and make the accented note stand out too far from the frame of its theme—the music would not "sit down," it would "fall down." But the elfin humor of this solitary sustained tone, pouncing mischievously on its unexpected chord, is admirably illuminated by an application of expressive color, a bright tone, with a rapid vibrato. As to its prolongation, the remainder of the bar, after it, is occupied by two sixteenth-notes. The first of these is one tone higher than the accented tone, thus being the root tone of the chord; the second is the same as the accented tone. The descending scale thus begun continues for the first three notes of the next bar; and the harmony of this next bar is the tonic, thus being a resolution of the dominant seventh harmony of the entire bar containing the accent; therefore the vitality of the accented tone must sing throughout its bar, not relaxing or coming to rest until its resolution on the beginning of the following bar. Also, the two sixteenth-notes which follow it are, properly understood, not so much upbeats to the ensuing phrase as they are an ornamented continuation of the accented note—a tiny upswing, returning to the main note. For all these reasons the accented tone must not be let go of before the next note is reached, and so a lengthening factor is called for. This interpretation will generally encounter some resistance on the part of the string players, as the most comfortable bowing includes a retake after the quarter-note, shortening it. But with a little effort the retake can be reduced to a negligible minimum.

It will be observed that Mendelssohn's accents, more than those of any other composer discussed in this survey, are expressive and not violent. Much of the reason for this fact is the suave style of his music in general; and yet, without abandoning it, he can also vividly suggest the surge of the surf in his wonderful *Hebrides Overture.* This inspired slice of nature painting is, as might be expected, copiously annotated by the composer with guides to nuances; often several simultaneous parts are meticulously marked differently. Many of those markings are accents; but here too, though, contrary to what might be expected, the accents are expressive rather than violent. As to the symbols for them, an examination of bars 252-4 (15-17 from the end) will prove that one cannot, in this work, profitably seek any distinction in meaning between them, except, as remarked previously, that Mendelssohn will write *sf*'s on several successive quarter-notes, but never on successive eighth-notes; in the latter case he will invariably resort to the more "plebeian" >.

The first six bars of the work are much alike, each one containing a calm statement of the unforgettable principal motive. In the third and fourth bars, the celli break off from the motive and give out a graceful counterpoint, suggesting a wave rolling lazily up on the beach. In the seventh and eighth bars, the principal motive suddenly vanishes, and the only moving voice is this counterpoint, heaving up in a substantial *crescendo* and *diminuendo,* and supported by a roll on the hitherto silent timpani. *(Fig. 45)* In the eighth bar, for the first time in the work, a quarter-note occurs on the second quarter of a bar. And this quarter-note, in addition, is tied over to the first sixteenth-note following—thus it is, except for the holding notes in the background, the longest note so far in the work; and it is accented. It is an E; the chord throughout the bar is E minor, having resolved from its dominant in the bar before; the main key being B minor, this is the first time either of these chords has been heard; and the instruments which have the accented note have on the first quarter of the bar two eighth-notes, E (the same as the accented note) and the B below.

In this pair of bars we have been given, for the first time in the work, an impression of something other than tranquillity. The "calm sea" motive is absent and the "restless sea" figure prevails—and in the *crescendo-diminuendo* with the rolling drums, the image of a mighty wave, reminding us of the power and terror of the sea, is swiftly conjured up. This "wave" reaches its height at the beginning of the eighth bar, and it would have been logical for the composer to have fixed his accent there, at which point the harmony also resolves. Yet he fixed it not there, but on the *next* quarter, on the repeated E *after* the resolution— to keep alive, and drive home, this stark, ominous tone. To make clear just how stark and ominous it is, one should observe that the chord in which it lies, the (minor) subdominant is always a dark shadow—and furthermore that that chord is preceded by its dominant, the tonic major—the sound of which, in a work in a minor key, is like a stab of cold steel.

As to the type of accent, then, we surely have color—not warm and soft, but cold and hard. So much of the surrounding music is smoothly flowing that an acute attack would not be fitting. A volume factor is possible if the volume is sustained throughout the tone. While the accented tone is really a quarter plus a sixteenth, one might suppose that it is already sufficiently lengthened to admit of no further lengthening; but this would not be true—the added sixteenth can indeed be sustained beyond the point to which it would be if not accented, and it seems that this should be done in the interests of sustaining this tone and maintaining the continuity of the melodic line. So the type is 23 or 26.

In the ninth through the fourteenth bars, the main motive reappears as before, though now continuously supported on a new running counterpoint. Suddenly the fifteenth bar is *forte,* without a preparatory *crescendo;* its third quarter is slurred to the preceding note and marked *"dim."* in all voices—and besides, the oboes, bassoons, and first violins are accented on the third quarter. The next bar begins *piano.* What kind of an accent is this? *(Fig. 46)*

Obviously, because of the slur, it cannot be acute. However, since this bar is a real *forte* and not a *crescendo in piano,* the volume factor is definitely in order. Color, too—though its purpose, and therefore its quality, is not clear. It could be to emphasize either the melodic line or the timbres of the instruments having the accent. At any rate, since the accented notes are also marked with the general *diminuendo,* the effect of the accent should exhaust itself in its first quarter's (the bar's third quarter's) value, and the accented voices should participate in the *diminuendo* on the bar's fourth quarter. The accent type will be 25.

The next accent to interest us is that in bar 23. *(Fig. 47)* A glance at the staves of the second violins, violas, celli, and basses shows that the dynamics at the point of this accent are *pianissimo,* or at most, *piano.* This should always be called to the attention of the winds and violins, who have the accent. Since the composer has marked *diminuendo* after the accent, volume should be a part of it—always remembering that the level to which this factor must be related is not *forte* but *piano.* Color, also, is an ingredient, and an acute attack could well be made here, as the simultaneous entrance of so many instruments is a calculated sonorous effect. The type is 16.

All the accents in the succeeding passage, up to the entrance of the second subject, are plain and expressive only. Obviously those in the second subject are too—how marvelously they invoke a sense of distance and longing, depicting the vast sweep to the horizon and the mystery of the seas and lands beyond! *(Fig. 48)* And they make one feel the human drama of the sea, a great compassion for the men who have been, and always will be, engulfed in its eternal depths.

In the *Italian Symphony* it will be sufficiently illustrative to examine a few accents in the second movement. The entrance of the horns and clarinets in this movement marks the beginning of the subsidiary theme; in some scores the letter at this point is A. This theme, in contrast to the severe main theme, is consolatory in character, and is built on a threefold rising sequence of a motive of three descending notes. The first of these three notes is always accented (according to previously stated principles, type 22 is best). The whole theme consists of a first phrase of four bars and a second one, much longer, with more active harmony (strangely beginning, too, with the subdominant immediately after a cadence on the dominant!) and fuller orchestration. In the first phrase the accents are marked >; in the second phrase they are marked *sf* on the first and third members of the sequence, and > on the second, as well as on a fourth, which pops up here.

(Fig. 49) But in the second phrase, the four members are not all ascending, as in the first phrase—the first and third are on the same pitch, and that is higher than the pitch of the second and fourth. The sense of the music, then, is that the first and third members make fresh starts, which hesitate with the second and fourth—or in other words, the first and third ask questions which the second and fourth answer. Ordinary musicianship would dictate a quality of greater intensity on the first and third than on the second and fourth, regardless of the accents; hence what Mendelssohn did with his accent marks was to (1) demonstrate his agreement with this conception of his music, and (2) call for the proper accentuation of the marked tones, each according to its context. All the accents in this theme should be of type 25, with a *diminuendo* on each accented note. The lengthening factor has not been included because, by definition, there is no place for it in the rhythmic pattern here. However, it is probably the most important factor generally in Mendelssohn's accents; virtually all of them have the sensation of wanting to "pull out" or "lean on" their note; and so, that being the general tendency, the performer should here be scrupulous to give the accented notes their full metrical value and even give them a subtle bit more, if he can do so without distorting the tempo, by way of an "agogic" accent.

The accents here, it has been pointed out, should be of type 25; and yet they are not all the same in sound. However, the difference between them is not in the accents themselves, but in the volume and intensity of tone upon which the accents are superimposed. The accents in the horns in bars 52 and 54 should not be overlooked, providing as they do a voice of weight and volume on the fourth quarter.

After a brief reprise of the main theme, this subsidiary theme returns. *(Fig. 50)* Now the leading parts are taken by the flutes in addition to the clarinets. All the accents in the first and second members of the sequence are now omitted, except a > in the first clarinet on its first note—of member one (and not in the first flute, which doubles the clarinet line an octave above!). Through member two there is, instead, a *crescendo;* and member three, in both flutes and clarinets, bears a *sf*. This combination of markings shows clearly that Mendelssohn's conception of his theme on its return was quite different from that on its first appearance. Here, the three distinct members of the first sequence have become welded into one continuous phrase. Instead of three fresh starts, each one with its stop, there is now a shy entrance (on the fourth quarter instead of, as before, the second) and a single line quickly mounting to the eloquent third member. Besides, each member, instead of drooping, now seems to rise, even though, as before, its three notes fall in pitch. Moreover, where there were rests in the inner voices at the theme's first appearance, now there are no rests— no relaxations of the music's destined progress. The accents here are similar to those of the previous appearance except as just noted and with slight differences besides, readily understood in the light of these remarks. Compare, for example, the first *forte* notes in both. In the return, this note comes on the beginning of the bar, while in the first appearance it had come on the third quarter; therefore in the return, it will naturally be more stressed, and Mendelssohn, cognizant of this, marked > on the first violin and cello-bass parts. At this point a lovely inner voice, in the second violins and a clarinet, rises and falls below the sustained tone in the top voice. In the first appearance of the theme this inner voice is not accented; but in the return the first note after the accented tone in the top voice, being also the highest note in the inner voice, is accented, but only in the clarinet part, not in the violins! And the former fourth quarter accents in the horns are here entirely omitted!

From Mendelssohn's procedure in this instance we can see how this fastidious craftsman delicately touched up his scores so as to produce many varieties and shades of stress and color from the subtlest to the most conspicuous, and how they lend themselves to the structure of his musical emotion.

Another illustrative accent in this movement is found in the second full bar in which there is no wind instrument playing—the eighth before letter A. It is the third bar of a transition theme in D minor that is closely derived from the main theme of the movement. *(Fig. 51)* For a bar it hovers around the note A, over dominant harmony, and then on the beginning of the following bar lands on a tonic triad; then it does this a second time. The first time, the melody note topping the tonic triad is D, the tonic itself; the second time, it is F, requiring a

longer skip to it; and it is this F that is accented, with a >. Discriminat-
ing interpreters rightly diagnose this accent as a plain one—of type 23
or 26, or a combination of 6 and 37. The first four bars of this theme
are then rounded off with a cadence, and the next phrase begins with
the same three bars as did the first phrase. In this occurrence of this
theme, the F's here referred to are the only accented notes.

This theme returns near the end of the movement, where the first
phrase is identical with its first occurrence, except that now the D which
begins the second bar is also accented, with a >; and this is so in the
second phrase as well. *(Fig. 52)* But then in the next bar of the second
phrase, where there had been an F in the melody before, there is now
an A, a whole octave above its predecessor, and its chord is a diminished
seventh instead of the previous placid tonic. And on this A there is a
sf, not only in the top voice (to which the other accents are confined)
but also in the next two voices beneath it. With this theme the elements
that create intensity are the culminating repetitions, the harmony, and
the size of the skip; and it is eminently right that the peak of the
theme is attained on a note that follows the last repetition and the
largest skip, and coincides with the most dramatic chord.

All the other accents in the theme, in both its appearances, are, in
quantity of accent force, one degree above the unaccented notes; but the
climactic accent is two degrees above—the accented D's in the latter occurrence of the theme, and the intensity the climactic note would have if
unaccented, are the first degree above the unaccented level, the "step-
ping stone" up to the peak. Surely a competent performer would play
the climactic note, with its dramatic chord, with some extra intensity
even if it carried no accent whatsoever. Then the written accent—regardless of which symbol is used—adds a further degree of something
to that. What the something will consist of depends on the musical
context, which at this point could well absorb an acute attack in addition to the other three factors comprised in the accent at the corresponding point in this theme's former appearance, this accent thus being
type 17. Mendelssohn gave us a direction to make some kind of an
accent, and a context from which we can judge which accent best fits
the frame. When he had done that, he had exhausted his authority as
well as his resources. The rest is up to us.

SEVEN

BRAHMS

From Mendelssohn to Brahms is the longest leap so far made in this survey, passing over, as it does, some mighty figures, including Schumann, Berlioz and Wagner. Significantly, the category that is skipped is the pinnacle of the Romantic movement; we have leaped from the ascent toward it to the descent beyond it without having touched the summit itself. This is more than sheer coincidence; for Schumann and Wagner, as well as various others of the movement, often resort to accents other than those in general acceptance, symbolized by the mark ∧; and we shall defer the discussion of them to the Appendix. Those accents of theirs which are indicated by the ordinary symbols are fully interpretable according to the procedures outlined in this survey; and since other Romantic composers are discussed herein, nothing would be gained by consuming space in the specific study ot their regular accents. One can rightly gather that the fever pitch of high romanticism calls for more vehement emphases than are comprised within the normal resources of accentuation, rich as they are. This is the one point at which art music breaks out of its self-imposed restraints and consequently needs additional symbols for the purpose of complete communication.

By the time Johannes Brahms had reached young manhood, the romantic movement in music had thoroughly recognized itself, and had been recognized by the public, for what it was. It was no longer obliged to plead or prove that the individual had the ability as well as the right to express his personal self. Its difficulty at that stage, though, was that of a military force that had conquered too far from its base: the farther it reached out the more attenuated had become its relation to its foundation and its source of strength and supply; if the progress it has made is to endure, the victory has to be consolidated and ample communication lines established with the base. Wagner, sensing this need, created *Die Meistersinger* as a glorious solution for the brave new world of music drama. However, the instrumental composers still lacked their champion, the One who would shiningly identify them as the authentic custodians of the sacred flame. No wonder they hailed Brahms' appearance on the scene. Schumann, with all his learned counterpoint, could not match Brahms' grandness of line, his somber nobility. Even Wagner himself—before all the "admirers" divided the musical world, so needlessly, into two hostile camps—recognized what the then young Brahms was doing, and generously predicted the place he would take in music. How fortunate it is that Brahms was a sufficiently stout and realistic character to remain unaffected by the prominence thrust upon him. He quietly remained, and developed, his gruff self; he did unify the advances music had made with the solid foundations; and in so fortifying those advances that were sound he caused, by his example, the specious ones to be more clearly perceived for what they were.

A concise sample of Brahms' art at its most mature and characteristic is readily available, and is entitled the *Tragic Overture*. At various points of its admirably homogeneous whole, it exhibits virtually all the features—consistent and contradictory—of its composer's musical idiom.

It is not essentially a melancholy piece; its title should be understood
in the Greek sense, of a drama which is serious, concerned with bas·c
truths, aware of the stern realities of existence, and not diverted from
proceeding to its destined conclusion. Moreover, Brahms gave the work
that title only a considerable time after having finished it, and even
then was not quite satisfied with the title.

It begins with two decisive chords, marked ff (except in the brass
and drums, which are f) and accented with ▼ symbols. Brahms rarely
used this symbol, and we can detect that when he did, he was asking for
a type of playing that fits his style perfectly: short and energetic but
heavy. His use of this symbol is the only special exception to his general
use of accents interpretable according to the general principles outlined
in this survey. One can imagine what a terrific crash he wanted in this
opening—a crash unfortunately never realized in performance, largely
because the trombones and tuba, which have much to do later, are
silent here. This observation leads to a related one: that Brahms was
invariably as careful about the visual appearance of his scores as he was
about their sound—occasionally to the latter's disadvantage. The causes
of this tendency were the strong conservative streak in his nature, and
his conscious mission as consolidator of the Romantic movement. He
leaned over backward to make it appear that there was nothing vulner-
ably new in his music; and he succeeded so well that, except where
absolutely required by the shape of his music, there is virtually nothing
in the appearance of his scores to differentiate his orchestral style from
Beethoven's. Although valved horns and trumpets were in general use in
his time, he stubbornly persisted in scoring for them on the fiction that
they were still handicapped (and blessed) by their archaic eighteenth
century construction. Harps and trombones had become standard members of the orchestra too recently for him to fully accept them as such,
and he always handled them with a certain diffidence, treating them
somewhat as extra-orchestral soloists. As his instincts were pure, he
doubtless felt that some of his contemporaries had gone too far in reducing the trombones from their formidable classic station to regular
hail-fellows-well-met of the orchestra. The maxim "exit in case of
Brahms," though happily no longer true of audiences, still applies to
most of the gentlemen of the percussion section. Producers of lush

sounds, such as the English horn and bass clarinet, were utterly ignored by Brahms throughout his career; however, it must be conceded that it would be difficult to find a proper place for them in his austere music. Yet to the extent that Brahms was meekly continuing a musical habit, or "following" a "tradition" (as with Mendelssohn in the instance cited previously), it must be said that the habit or "tradition" was an illusory, or at best a vestigial, one. Bach's and Handel's brass parts are highly melodic (the virtually percussive style of brass writing is what it degenerated into in the latter eighteenth century); Bach often wrote for his equivalent of the English horn, and Mozart's mature operas contain prominent parts for basset horn, which is almost halfway from the clarinet to the bass clarinet. As Brahms doubtless knew, there was ample precedent for all the instrumental uses that he denied himself. Why, then, did he deny them to himself? The answer lies partly in the formal cast of his music, partly in his desire to forestall stupid criticism, and partly in his strong sense of belonging intensely to his age and that immediately preceding—so intensely that he felt impelled to adopt its formulae, even the arbitrary ones, even the obviously misconceived ones. Schubert, Schumann, and Mendelssohn, as well as Beethoven, limited their use of the brass to its highly restricted compass of the later eighteenth century, and were almost as cautious with percussion, despite the new developments in that department. But Schubert, Schumann, Berlioz, and Mendelssohn far outdid Brahms in the freedom, confidence, and color of their writing for the trombones—except in the *Second Symphony,* where Brahms' trombone writing is as brave and "romantic" as anybody's. His use of accent symbols, like everything else in his scoring, is traditional and imitative. With him all the symbols (always excepting the $\blacktriangledown$) are fully interchangeable. Exhaustive study has failed to expose any one set of circumstances under which Brahms either always or never uses any given one of his symbols.

As we look again at the *Tragic Overture,* the first two chords are followed by four bars of a ghostly theme, the largest and most significant part of which consists of quarter-notes that glide smoothly by. *(Figs. 53-54)* The tempo is *allegro, alla breve*. In the seventh and eighth bars, for the first time since the initial two chords, accents occur—and the pulse becomes one of solid half-notes. The situation suggests an obvious parallel, of similar description, in the sixth bar of this work's companion piece, the *Academic Festival Overture.* Oddly enough, too, both passages are marked *"sotto voce,"* an unusual direction in Brahms, indicating a shadowy, mysterious color. In the *Academic Festival Overture* the first five bars do not glide by like the beginning of the *Tragic Overture,* but they bustle in eighth-notes over a bass bouncing in quarters. In both cases the effect of the sudden appearance of the half-notes is to pull the motion up short. If this impression were not counteracted by some newly added ingredient, the feeling of spontaneity and conviction, as well as the sense of movement, would falter. The device with which Brahms "turns defeat into victory" is the accent—which he attaches to all four half-notes in these two bars, in the *Tragic Overture,* and to both half-notes in the one bar of the *Academic Festival Overture.* With the accent he also gives "edge" to his typical salty harmonies, as well as adds a touch of excitement to the pre-existing mystery—a hint of "ah!" to the silent question, "what's going on?" Try to imagine these bars without their accents, and it will be apparent how much difference the accents make. There is, however, one difference between the accents in the two overtures: in the *Academic Festival Overture,* the accented half-notes come at the end of a phrase and form a cadence; and the dynamics are continuously *pianissimo.* It would be uncalled for to include the volume or color factor in these accents—either one would dispel the mysterious or "gray" atmosphere which is intended to continue for still quite some time; therefore we have here an accent of type 8. In the *Tragic Overture,* the accented half-notes introduce a new figure, and immediately precede one bar in which a *crescendo* from *piano* to *forte* must be made. Since, therefore, the "gray" section is ended for the time being and an energetic section is coming quickly (but with a *crescendo,* not *subito*), a vitalizing color would be proper in these accents in addition to the factors included in the other overture—*viz.,* type 14. Owing to the melodic figure, the first violins, violas, and first bassoon have their half-notes only on the first half of the bars; but the shorter notes that they do have should carry the same accent nonetheless, and be sustained for their full value—as well as the dotted eighth- and sixteenth-notes which form the upbeats to both accented bars. The reason for the lengthening factor is found in two data: the title of the work, which rules out any suggestions of gayety, surely at least at the beginning; and the entrance of the bassoons at the accented bars. Bassoons are not the instruments one would especially select for the purpose of imparting a light touch to the proceedings, and we may be sure that that could not have been Brahms' object here. To play any notes in these bars *staccato,* is, therefore, to thwart the many and unanimous indications in the score.

As to the orchestral technique, the *sotto voce* sections of both overtures will normally be played by the strings with the bow crossing the strings near the fingerboard to darken their tone a bit. But in the *Tragic Overture,* when the accented half-notes appear, with their upbeat, the bow should shift toward the bridge into ordinary position, or even slightly nearer the bridge than that, to facilitate the bow getting a good grip on the strings, and to impart definition to the tone.

The next accents occur on the fourth quarter of bar 10, the second and fourth quarters of bar 11, and the second of bar 12. *(Fig. 54)* Thus they cause a sustained syncopation such as Brahms indulges in much oftener than any other important composer. Here the only note heard in the orchestra is A, a unison dominant pedal. The winds and basses leap an octave upward at each accented place, holding each A for the two quarters between leaps. The violins have a sustained tremolo in sixteenth-notes on A's in octaves, their accents being in the same places as the rest of the orchestra's. Now, firstly, of which type shall the winds' and basses' accents be? Obviously, whichever it be, it must include an acute attack. The volume factor, except possibly on the initial "bite," seems excluded by the fact that a restatement of the "ghostly" theme, played *fortissimo* by the full orchestra, follows these accented notes directly, and the *fortissimo* should not be anticipated. Color is not called for either, since these bars are nothing but a syncopated preparation for a restatement of the theme; expressive intensity and featured instrumental timbre are both irrelevant. Lengthening might be desired, by way of intensifying the "eager" character of the dominant pedal A, if it were not that the attack on each syncopated A will be more telling if a normal space, as in the case of an unaccented note, is allowed before each. Therefore it is seen that the type that is called for here is either 1 or 2. As for the violins, it is obviously impossible for them to play a sustained accent. However, they could conceivably impart an extra emphasis to each group of eight notes that they play. The objection to this is that this way only their first accent would be heard, for if they were to play all the remaining iterated notes alike, their second, third, and fourth accents would disappear. Therefore the first of their every eight notes must have something more than the succeeding seven. It could also be the first two or three, etc., if it were not for the consideration that the vital spot is just the very beginning of each accent, because of the prominent syncopation. Accordingly the violins' accent also should be either type 1 or type 2, and on only the first of each eight repeated notes.

The next accents occur in bars 21-22. *(Fig. 55)* Bar 20 consists of two decisive chords which form a cadence with their resolution on the first beat of bar 21. But this resolution is not a full chord—it is a grim and muscular unison on D, the tonic; and it is also the beginning of a fierce new theme. The melody of this theme is in the violins and violas, and its first bar is an ascending figure with the rhythm of a dotted quarter-note and five eighth-notes, all detached, with a *crescendo* on the latter half of the bar extending into the next bar. Meanwhile the rest of the orchestra, part of it with a *crescendo,* sustains its D for a half bar, then fans out into some of Brahms' typical "gritty" harmonies. The first accent lies on the first note of bar 21, and solely in the violin and viola parts.

The energetic character of the music surely calls for an acute attack. As to the volume factor, it must be observed that the last dynamics direction these instruments had is *fortissimo,* and a further *crescendo* immediately following is indicated. A volume factor in this accent would require the violins and violas to play *fff* with a *crescendo* on top of that; this is sufficiently unreasonable to be dismissed as unintended, and hence we shall exclude it. As to color, the omission of harmony is itself a highly expressive device, creating (when adequately realized, of course) a character that can be described as stark and stormy. Such a color, then, should be imparted to the tone of the violins and violas, along with a rugged quality by bowing near the frog. As to the lengthening factor, it seems beyond question that it should be included; for its omission would not only allow the sustained D's in the other parts (some with *crescendo,* besides!) to sound through with disproportionate force, thus attracting the listener's attention to matters of secondary importance, but it would also bring about an unmusical rupture of the melodic line which would thwart its natural direction. It is obvious that, notwithstanding that every note must be independently articulated, the tone must be kept fully alive into the first eighth-note. So the accent here is type 14.

The other accent in this bar is more complicated. It lies in all the parts other than violins and violas, on the third quarter, as follows: flutes and trumpets, after a silent half bar; other woodwinds and horns, on tones of a chord reached *legato* and *crescendo* from the unison D; timpani, on the second of the two rolled half-notes, the first of which also bears a *crescendo;* celli and basses, on the second of two half-notes which are not slurred together, and the first of which bears neither a *crescendo* nor any other expression mark. All the notes affected by this accent are half-notes, and they are all tied to the same notes, also half-notes, in the next bar.

Let us consider first the horns, and woodwinds other than flutes. Their attack cannot be an acute one, because their accented notes are reached by slurs from the note before. The presence of the volume factor is equally clearly required by the fact that the accented notes are approached with a *crescendo.* The duration factor is excluded by the fact of the accented notes' being tied to their successors. The color factor remains for consideration; and while the conscious application of expressive and/or instrumental color to the mass of sound already established would make hardly any perceptible difference—to be candid about it—let us examine this point nonetheless for whatever it will add to our understanding of the passage. The scoring of this chord —a diminished seventh, be it noted—places the flutes and oboes in their most audible registers; while the clarinets and bassoons go *down* from the "unison" D to their lowest and thickest registers, and the second horn descends a full octave to its lowest possible note, bass D. Considering all these data, it appears that Brahms wanted something more from these instruments than to merely support the melody—he also wanted them to be heard as themselves, with their special timbres. Therefore it seems fully justified to include the color factor here. It can be brought out by rehearsing the wind instruments alone, letting them clearly hear themselves, and directing them to make their tones penetrate with full awareness of their desired role. So far, then, we have type 25.

However, as pointed out above, the violins and violas have a *crescendo* in the latter half of this bar extending into the next bar. Then they attain the climax of their phrase on the third quarter of that next bar—and it is accented (of this more below). And on that third quarter, the winds change their chord, to another half-note. Whether or not they were intended to be prominently heard, they must somehow adjust themselves to what the violins and violas are doing. Whether their place is above or below the surface, they have to maintain it, whatever it is, because the violins and violas could not have been meant to emerge gradually into relative prominence as they approach the climax of their phrase. Their tone grows, but not at the expense of the rest of the orchestra. Accordingly the wind instruments we are now considering should make a *crescendo* with the violins. But since they are already blowing *fortissimo,* they shall have to make a quick drop in volume and then increase again in volume and intensity through the first half of bar 22. Their accent thus is seen to be a compound one, of class E—first one from class B rounded off with one from class C: the most appropriate one of which is most probably type 36. As a result of this process, carried through according to the same principles followed in every other case, the conclusion that a class E accent is called for is plainly arrived at.

As to the flutes, which enter after a half rest, it seems best to adjust their accent to that of the other winds we have discussed. Even though they are fully capable of making an acute attack, their doing so would be in something less than the best musical effectiveness, as we shall see by studying the melody once again. This melody progresses in a direct line to its apex in the second bar; the apex itself is the only proper point of bearing down hard, for if one does so at a previous point the "flight" of the theme will be more or less bogged down. The accent we have described so far for this point is the heaviest it will bear.

It should be further mentioned, as regards the flutes, that whenever flutes double other instruments at the octave, as here, the more perfectly they are in tune the less they will be heard themselves, and the more they will help the instruments *which they are doubling* to be clearly heard. The cause of this phenomenon is that in such cases the flutes merely slip into an already existing overtone of the lower instrument, but in so doing they give it a "boost" which carries along with it the fundamental tone of the lower instrument.

Proceeding farther down the score, we come to the trumpets, which, like the flutes, have entered, with an accent, on the second half of the bar. Their last dynamic mark was *forte*. For the reasons stated above, an acute attack is not desired here, but color is—the two trumpets have their low D in unison, and that is a dramatic sound indeed. But as mentioned before, the winds here must not only assert their own colors but also serve as support to the violins and violas. If the trumpets enter *forte* they will not only stand out from the woodwinds, not blending with them, but also have to blow too loudly when it comes time for them to participate in the *crescendo* behind the violins and violas. Therefore it would seem best for them to enter *mf,* make the most of their color, and then make a *crescendo*. Their unison D carries over through the first half of the next bar, and then on the third quarter they have a quarter-note A in octaves. But the beat on which this quarter-note falls is the climactic one of the whole two-bar motive. The trumpeters, of course, cannot discover that from anything they can see in their parts. Therefore they will naturally make a brief rest between their D and A. Nothing will more effectively kill the climax than just this. Accordingly they should be told to keep the tone, with the *crescendo,* alive until they reach the A. In our scheme this amounts to another compound accent, of class E, the types included being 22 and 37.

Now—still on the second half of bar 21—descending the score farther, we come to the timpani. This part, for these two bars, consists of three half-notes and a quarter-note, with a roll on all but the last, a *crescendo* on the first half-note, and an accent on the second. The pre-existing dynamics are *forte,* although the indication of this is not explicit. After the *crescendo* on the first half-note, the accented note is reached with the dynamics in the timpani already *fortissimo*. A further increase in volume would cover the melody. But the timpanist has other

devices with which to increase intensity on his instrument: he can raise
the frequency of beats in his roll, and he can strike his drum nearer its
edge, thus making each beat more clearly audible. The timpanist should
effectuate this accent in both these ways, making a slight *diminuendo*
at the end of the bar so as to allow for a slight *crescendo* toward the
end of the roll without covering the rest of the orchestra.

Finally we come to the celli and basses, which have a half-note D,
then an accented half-note tied over to a continuation of the same notes
in the next bar for a half-note. On the accented note the basses simply
repeat their lowest D, but the celli, whose first D was an octave above
their lowest D, leap down to that lowest D and couple it with a higher
harmony note, in a double stop. Color will be part of this accent, as it
is in the rest of the orchestra. The duration factor is not involved, as
the note is tied over. As to "bite" and volume, these factors had better
depend on the balance resulting from the directions already set forth.
Much will depend on the bowing with which the accented notes are
sounded. In any case, the tone should not be allowed to flag at any
point in the second bar, bar 22 of the overture.

This observation brings us to the last accent we shall examine in this
passage, the one on the climactic note in the violins and violas. The
note is a dotted quarter, and it is tied to the note to which it resolves,
an eighth-note, which stands at the end of the bar. In the following
bar (23) the basses, celli, and bassoons take over the violin-viola theme
of the two preceding bars, in inversion. As the accented climactic note
is discordant, and one of the two longest notes in the theme, it is the
expressive center of gravity and, as such, needs an acute attack, volume,
and expressive color (it would also have a lengthening factor if it were
not tied to the next note)—type 16. The eighth-note after it, while not
accented, must continue to carry vitality and tension to the very last
drop, to pass it over to the basses, celli, and bassoons.

For the only place where this theme reappears, see bars 171 ff., where
an excellent illustration is afforded also of the interchangeable way in
which Brahms uses his accent symbols.

There is much tempting food for thought in this work, which it would
be better to pass by because similar problems have been dealt with elsewhere. However, before we leave it let us look at a passage near the

end, beginning with bar 395. *(Fig. 56)* Firstly, there is the accented note at the beginning of the bar. The theme in which it occurs is the opening "ghostly" one, and the instant figure is one that has occurred several times previously in the work (*e.g.* bars 61 ff.). But observe the difference in orchestration: previously only the celli were given triple stops to play, whereas here—the last time the figure recurs in the work except for bars 401-2—every section of strings, *including the basses* (!) has triple stops (what a grand *kräftig* German touch!). At the last previous appearance of this figure the winds join in, but while the strings are marked *sff* in these bars, the winds have only the regular *sf*. The additional number of strings being vibrated, and the heavy hand on the bows necessary to set them in vibration, would alone make these accents larger than their prior counterparts. But Brahms doubtless believed he had to show that his intentions agreed with this result—so he marked the strings *sff*. The accents are, of course, type 16. Now the climax of the overture as a whole occurs in the first half of bar 397. This point is the fourth note of an augmentation of the "ghostly" theme, in the wind instruments alone. All these instruments have a series of accented half-notes except the third trombone and tuba, which have a descending scale in quarter-notes, unaccented. However, when they reach the climactic chord, they also have a half-note, and it is accented. The harmony of each of these half-notes is as follows: D minor, B flat major, G minor, dominant seventh of A. How mighty, and unexpected-inevitable, this last chord is! What a sudden and glorious burst of G sharp and B natural! But this does not make it an escape from the tragedy—it makes it, instead, the tragedy's culmination and fulfillment, the terrible moment of illumination wherein all becomes instantly and starkly clear.

This accent has to have everything: "bite," dynamics, lengthening, and color—type 17. Not only that—since it is on one of the grandest chords in musical literature, that chord should also be preceded by a *rubato* broadening in the tempo—not much, of course, only just right. The rest is just tying up the threads; and from this point on, even though the work ends with a page of *fortissimo,* the trombones are no longer heard. They have served their appointed purpose.

And so has their master. In at least one way Brahms was the ideal creative artist: he combined a vast and original creative impulse with a profound reverence for precedent, a vivid sense of the validity of artistic progress by evolution, not revolution. His was a rich musical mind—it knew stark, sinewy strength as well as melting tenderness; and his handling of his material—including, decidedly, his use of accents—is a subject whose study will yield rich rewards.

EIGHT

CHAIKOVSKY

Chaikovsky follows Brahms in chronological order—not solely, or even primarily, because of the seven years that separated their births, nor despite the fact that Brahms outlived him. Indeed, in some ways, Brahms' music is more "modern" than Chaikovsky's—if by "modern" one refers to the capacity of an art work to communicate something vital, directly to the public of the present time, without requiring that public to adjust itself to the "form and pressure" of an earlier era. Essentially Chaikovsky properly follows Brahms because (regardless of the aesthetic merit of his work) his music displays an exploration of tonal resources more free, more daring, and farther beyond the horizon of the classic masters than Brahms'—largely self-imposed though Brahms' may have been—and thus if he is no nearer today in his work, at least he is farther away from the origins. It comes as a surprise to learn that one of the supreme objects of Chaikovsky's adulation was Mozart; but this paradox can be explained by the interpretation that the qualities Chaikovsky appreciated in Mozart were not only the effortless perfection, the purity, the serene grace, but also the intense singing line, the nervous vitality, the harmonic richness, the colorful orchestral palette, the powerful character delineation in the operas. He refused to consider the disparity between their character, of which he was well aware, an obstacle to genuine understanding and sympathy.

In Chaikovsky, music reached a new high (or, perhaps, low) in "sound and fury." He tears passion to tatters as it had never been torn before—or, for that matter, since, with few possible exceptions. His music is richly kaleidoscopic, red-blooded, "juicy"; his melodies, magnificent as many of them are, tend to drip treacle up to the point of nausea; he juxtaposes, often with brilliant success, remote harmonies. With these resources he has left us much that is powerfully stirring, much that is daintily captivating, and much that is deservedly forgotten or almost forgotten, because it either packs too much of a wallop, or is devoid of communicative significance. He is a pure romantic—he leans heavily on rhetoric; and when it fails of its effect there is too little solid composition sustaining it. His music cannot be treasured by those to whom balance, restraint, order, and good taste are paramount.

As with many other important composers, his creative output comprises works which aim to plumb the profundities of human experience, as well as works intended simply for pleasant entertainment. The latter category includes a sizable library of masterly and perennial scores written for the ballet, of which the *Nutcracker* is probably the most popular. This music is colorful, and constantly ingratiating. The concert suite extracted from the complete ballet score opens with an "Ouverture Miniature" in which no instrument lower than the violas appears, nor do the trumpets or trombones. The violins and violas are divided throughout; and they begin *pianissimo,* in a 2-4 time signature. *(Fig. 57)* The third bar has an accent, marked >, on its first note in all parts. The chord is the subdominant, in the first inversion, immediately resolving to the tonic, but the rhythmic movement continues in eighth-notes. To interpret this accent as one of force would be contrary to everything in the context; it is like a little curtsy in this smiling phrase, and the type should be 6 or 22. The accent in the next bar is on the dominant ninth of the dominant; its value is a full quarter, and then it resolves to the dominant, gracefully closing off the first four-bar phrase. Accordingly it is a weightier point than that of the preceding accent, and a slight dynamic pressure in addition to a gentle warm color would be in order—type 25. The next accent is on the last note of the sixth bar (the second bar of the second four-bar phrase). If this accent were not there, the pulse of every one of the first eight bars, and their repetition, which occurs immediately, would fall squarely on all the heavy beats. Thus the main effect of this accent is to vary slightly the rhythmic uniformity. It will accomplish this with another type 25 accent; one with an acute factor would be beyond the scope of this theme and the orchestration. Signs of bustling appear in the fluttering voice of the violas, and they amount to some agitation in the woodwind material that follows. The violins then intrude with a querulous figure—three repeated sixteenth-notes, then a five-note descending scale; this is answered in the woodwinds. *(Fig. 58)* There is an accent on the first note of the scale, which is also the first note of the bar. Other strings and woodwinds sustain the harmony for their respective leading voices, and their first notes are also accented. Here, since the music is getting quite busy and harmonically varied, an acute factor is called for as well as expressive emphasis, and the accents should be of type 16; care being taken in the sustaining parts that the accent tone will evaporate after only one sixteenth-note's value. A refinement of this interpretation would be to let the influence of the accent carry over into one or more of the notes of the scale immediately following, producing a *diminuendo* of intensity rather than an abrupt termination of it. This would be even more musically proper than confining the accent strictly to the one note to which it belongs —as well as easier and more natural for both good and poor musicians to play.

The woodwind accents in bars 35 and 36 are on the same music as that of the beginning of the piece, and the same considerations apply to them. The decorative fluttering in the violins does not affect the return to the mood as well as the thematic material of the opening.

In bar 41 there are two interesting accents, both marked *sf*—the first appearance of this symbol in the work. The first of these is on a high G of both oboes, on the beginning of the bar, and sustained throughout three and three-quarter bars. *(Fig. 59)* The dynamics have reached *forte,* and the oboes have the field to themselves for the first three-quarters of a bar. The effect here is obviously one purely of instrumental timbre, and hence there must be a color factor in the accent.

There should also be a marked attack. A volume factor would tend to make the sound of the oboes ugly; and since a loud sound is not what is intended here (or else the composer would have added more instruments), but just a bright or "cute" effect, the accent should be type 13.

The strings then enter with six pairs of quickly resolving discords and resolutions, all in eighth-note movement, each discord situated off the beat, marked *sf,* and slurred to its resolution which falls on the beat. Now a good look at the passage will show us that each chord of resolution should be less loud than the discord which resolves to it; hence there should be a volume factor in the accent. Also this string entrance comes at the culmination of a short passage of increasing restlessness; for this reason, as well as to balance the accent of the oboes, an acute attack should be included. The charm of the movement and the sameness of all these pairs of chords call for expressive color also. The accent is hence of type 16.

The accents in bars 55 and 56 *(Fig. 60)* are obviously purely expressive; and a lovely interpretation of them would be an accent of class C, say, 36, taking the form of a quick *crescendo* and a less quick *diminuendo.* The next accents, in bars 61, 63, 65, 67, and 69, are especially interesting ones. *(Fig. 61)* They all occur in identical rhythm patterns: a dotted quarter, then sixteenth-notes for the remainder of each pair of bars; and the dotted quarters are accented with the symbol >. Also, every one of the dotted quarters is bare of accompaniment for a whole quarter's duration. The first of these accented notes has the word *grazioso* written over it. It and the second are *piano,* but between them there is a *crescendo.* So we have the rare but perfectly logical case of an accented note being in a lower dynamic category than an adjacent (here, preceding) unaccented note. If the volume factor were included in the accent, the composer's manifest intention would be thwarted. How else, then, should the accent be effectuated? Firstly, the composer has given an explicit hint with the word *grazioso*. An acute attack would contravene this character. Thus far in this piece the duration factor has not been involved, since every accented note before this one has been slurred to its successor. But here such is not the case, and the duration factor is available. As has been pointed out, the first two of these accents are in *piano;* the third is *mp,* the fourth, *mf,* and the fifth, *f*. And the third and fourth are higher in pitch than the first two, and the last is higher yet. Thus the passage is one of increasing intensity, and it will help to make it sound so if each accented note is sustained longer than the preceding one; and as the last one is the climax of the theme, it could very well also have an acute attack. Accordingly the accent type on the first accented note should be 22; on the second, third, and fourth, 23; and on the fifth, 14.

The last accent to be considered in this "Ouverture Miniature" is found in bars 80 and 82, in all the wind parts. *(Fig. 62)* It is on a quarter-note, in *forte;* and the preceding bar, in which the figure to which this note belongs begins, is marked *pesante* in all the wind parts. Again, the composer has given us the key explicitly, though, as before, it might well have been deduced from the context. Force, weight and duration are the factors called for here, so the accent type is 26.

The first piece in the suite, following the "Ouverture Miniature," is a March. It opens with its main theme in the winds, *piano,* except for the last note of its second bar, a half-note, on which the phrase "sits down" in *mezzo-forte* with a *diminuendo*. *(Fig. 63)* The first two bars are then literally repeated. There follows an extended principal section, then a contrasting middle section, and a return to the opening material, in fuller scoring than at the beginning, and in *forte;* and in the return, the note which at the beginning had been marked *mf dim.* is now marked *sf dim*. *(Fig. 64)* Considering all these data, it appears that the accented note, in order to preserve the original relationship of the notes of the theme, must be louder than the others—and hence we have the volume factor. The character is energetic, and so an acute attack is indicated. Vitality should also appear in the tone color. The duration of the tone, however, should be no longer than at the beginning, for the commencement of the following two-bar phrase must still be freshly articulated. An important practical consideration, so often honored in the breach, is that the *diminuendo* on the accented tone must be fast and extensive in order that the downrush of the flutes against it can be heard. The accent type is 16.

After the March comes the imaginative but somewhat cloying "Dance of the Sugar-Plum Fairy," noted for its introduction of the celesta, but perhaps more interesting for its succulent use of the bass clarinet. The first accents in it occur in bars 17 and 18, on sustained chords, *piano,* in the woodwinds, which are slurred to their successors. *(Fig. 65)* These chords are all prefaced by little runs in the clarinets which imitate the motive previously introduced on the bass clarinet; but while on the bass clarinet the motive had introduced a four-bar phrase, here the first bar of that phrase is treated as a one-bar motive in sequence four times, to round out the first sixteen-bar period. This difference calls for nothing but expressive intensity, as the harmonic and structural tension increases to the end of the period; so the accents should be type 22 or 23.

In bar 20, the prevailing dynamic level is *mf,* the loudest it has been so far. On the last eighth-note of this bar numerous instruments enter, to produce a startling percussive effect as well as to introduce the dominant pedal point for the middle section of the movement, which begins here. The note of the winds is detached, while that of the strings is tied over into the next bar, where it is marked *pp*. Every voice is marked *sf* at the inception of this note; and since every voice after that inception is marked *pp,* the dynamic shock is intentional, and therefore the accent must be such as to effectuate it accordingly. The flutes are the only instruments whose parts have a *staccato* dot, but for them to play *staccato* while everyone else who interjects this note plays it sustained, would be absurd. The conductor must decide whether all play it shortened, lengthened, or normal duration; according to that decision, the accent type will be 10, 11, or 12.

There are interesting accents in bars 23 and 24 *(Fig. 65),* all indicated by the symbol >. Starting at the bottom of the score, the violas have a triplet rhythm, in *piano,* the first note of which is tied to its successor, and accented. The harmony, together with the new viola figure, suggests some anxiety; the choice of the violas, with their nervous, "woody" tone, instead of, for instance, the equally available celli, indicates further a rather sinister tone quality. The prominence of the English horn, whose accent will be discussed below, gives additional evidence of the intended prevailing color. Accordingly, the dark quality of the viola tone should be brought out; but the shortness of the note allows little opportunity for the accent to be realized without additional factors. The "bite" of the violas on their lower strings does provide the very color desired; therefore in bar 23 the accent should be 3 or 13. The harmony of that bar is active, while that of bar 24 is cadential, in which the tension is somewhat relaxed; so in the latter bar it seems best to leave the accent merely a plain one, of type 6 or 22.

Going up the page, we come next to the second and fourth horns, also *piano,* sustaining the outer tones of the chords for a dotted quarter, accented. Surely one purpose of the accent is to add to the tone's duration, and thus to contrast that chord with the one on the remaining eighth of the bar, the dominant of the next bar's first chord, which, being a mere upbeat, must be lighter than either principal chord. The choice of the horns for the supporting harmony here is a felicitous one: horns can have a commanding timbre, or none at all, depending on their register, dynamics, and function. Here in their lower middle register, in *piano,* they are heard not really as horns, but just as neutral background; and there is no cause for their timbre to be featured. But as has been said, the short note at the end of the bar must be lighter than the long note; and so, of the many possible ways of making the long note heavier, in addition to giving it its full duration, the most appropriate here would be to give the one in the first of these two bars an acute attack, to properly support the violas, and also a sustained vital tone—type 14. Then in the second bar the horns should have the same minus the acute attack—type 23.

Now for the English horn, which enters on the second eighth of both bars, on the leading tone of each chord, proceeding *legato* to the tonic on the third eighth. In the first of the two bars the dynamics are *mf,* and in the second, *p;* and the leading tone in both bars is accented.

This is the only voice in which the dynamics are marked differently in the two bars; and the difference confirms the relative repose of the second bar, which we had discovered from the musical structure alone. What this instrument does in these two bars is just to add a lugubrious "O.K." to each triad already formed elsewhere. An acute factor in this accent would produce a comic effect inconsistent with that produced by the other instruments, and therefore we must reject it. But as this is this instrument's first solo entrance in the whole work, it is reasonable to infer that the composer was holding its characteristic tone color in reserve for just this moment; and to carry out his intention we must apply the color factor. There is no question of any duration factor as the accented note is slurred to its successor in both bars. This leaves the volume factor to be considered. The normal phrasing in this case, even if there were no accent, would involve some lessening of stress as the leading tone is quitted for the tonic; and it would be absurd to believe that the composer intended some manner of execution which would thwart this normal nuance. And considering the accent, we may well deduce that he even intended this normal nuance to be exaggerated; and on this supposition we decide that a volume factor should be present. Accordingly, the type is 25.

The next movement, the "Danse Russe Trepak," is sheer exuberant athletic fun, and at least one of its enjoyers wishes there were a good deal more of it. It starts off with a merry leap by the full orchestra, save for brass and percussion, and immediately continues *piano* for the remainder of its opening two-bar motive. *(Fig. 66)* The second bar is built on the supertonic seventh chord, and the middle note of the bar is marked *sf*. The third and fourth bars comprise a sequence of the first two, but at the point in the fourth bar corresponding to the accented note of the second bar, the chord is the tonic and not accented. On the accented chord the woodwinds have also a *staccato* dot, the violins are slurred to their next notes, and the other instruments, which have just that one detached note, are unmarked other than by the *sf*. Let us study what this might be. As for color of any kind, there seems no reason, or indeed opportunity, for it in this animated rhythmic movement. But an acute attack certainly seems in order, as does the volume factor, which would still leave considerable difference in loudness between the accented *piano* note and the *forte* chords nearby. As to the duration factor, the context admits of either lengthening, to make for weight, or shortening, to make for brightness of rhythm—this question is up to each conductor, and it must be carefully thought through, because many similar accents throughout the movement will largely determine the entire character of the piece. The type, then, will be either II or I2.

The first sixteen-bar period is then repeated, *ff,* with the addition of the brass and percussion, the *piano* of the opening being also duly increased to *mf.* The accent recurs as at the beginning, and either solution of the duration problem will be just as valid here as it had been there.

In the repetition, an inner voice, moving in quarter notes, has each note accented with the symbol >. At the beginning, in *piano,* this voice was in the woodwinds, unaccented, and slurred; *(Fig. 66)* but here it is in the horns and detached. If we needed a guide to this accent as to the duration factor, it would be provided by the former legato phrasing of this voice. The boisterous music calls for an acute attack, and the rollicking ring of the horns would be well brought out with a color factor, so their accent would be type 14. The principal voice of the middle section of the piece lies in the basses; and its second and fourth bars each consist of two quarter-notes, marked >. *(Fig. 67)* It should require no discussion to show that these quarter notes should be quite heavy—long, acute, and solid, type 17. Significantly enough, the canonic imitation of this voice in the woodwinds is not accented, but the quarter-notes are marked with a line for breadth.

The return of the first section is *ff* throughout, and the previous orchestration is enlarged by a tambourine. While the accent in the second bar is, as before, marked *sf,* the tambourine part is accented with the symbol >. If Chaikovsky had any inkling of any difference in the quality of accents owing to the different symbols, we cannot divine what it might have been. Now the inner voice in the horns should have the same accent as before, plus a volume factor, making the type 17; and this also applies to the trombones when they join the horns in the *fff* coda.

The next movement, the "Danse Arabe," is a superb tone painting

of a vast, arid desert waste, with a completely (though perhaps diaph-
anously) veiled torso undulating sinuously to the wailing of an
oriental reed pipe. After four monotonous bars of rhythmic introduction on an open fifth, G-D, in the muted strings—which continues
virtually throughout the piece, the clarinets and English horn enter
piano on an F major triad, resolving it to a G minor third. *(Fig. 68)*
This combination of harmonies intensifies the "parched" sound of
either one alone; and with an accent, symbolized by > over each F
major triad, the composer must have been hoping for such an effect to
be still further emphasized. The orchestration of this chord throws
further light on how the accent is to be effectuated. Since the chord
naturally consists of three notes, there must be three instruments to
play it. The scoring of this movement includes a bass clarinet in addition to the two regular clarinets; and one must ask why the composer
used the English horn instead of the bass clarinet for one of the three
voices, especially since the clarinets play in their low register, with
which the bass clarinet would fit in perfectly. The only possible answer
is timbre—the desolate sound of the English horn, unmistakably lim-
ning the "lone and level sands stretching far away." The clarinets
should match that tone as much as possible, stressing not their tone's
body, but its hollowness and reediness. This can be achieved if the
clarinetists will place their mouthpieces so that a little less of them
than usual will be inside their mouths, and then pinch them in their
embouchures somewhat more tightly than normal. The languid character of the movement seems to reject the idea of acuteness in this
accent; but a volume factor seems right for the foreign harmony of the
accented chord before it resolves to its consonant successor. The type,
then, is 25.

Presently the violins enter with a drowsy melody in thirds. *(Fig. 69)*
Its fourth bar starts with a double passing tone, of one-eighth value,
marked with a *staccato* dot, followed on the next eighth beat by its
resolution, a consonant third, still monotonously G minor; but whereas
before in the woodwinds the G minor resolution had been reached
legato and on the last eighth of the bar, here it is attacked detached on
the second eighth. And here it is the resolution, not the resolving chord,
that is accented. To complete the description of the spot, the violins

entered *piano, molto espress.,* muted, and at the point of the accented note they are marked *più f.* To address ourselves now to the analysis of this accent, the accented note, a quarter-note, is a clear syncopation, with the rhythmic displacement quite pronounced. A volume factor would serve to carry out this effect. A lengthening factor is also required, to give sufficient emphasis to the accented note, and also to keep the melodic line from becoming broken. From the direction *"molto espress."* we can be sure that the accented note, above all, must receive the expressive value. An acute attack would impair the mood; and thus the accent type is 26. The remainder of the accents in this movement and the "Danse Chinoise" should be clearly comprehensible in the light of this analysis.

The "Danse des Mirlitons" is a dainty movement featuring the orchestra's flute trio. There is an odd accent in the fourth bar of their part. *(Fig. 70)* They move in sixteenth-notes throughout the third bar and, at the beginning of the fourth, land on a quarter-note, forming the subdominant minor triad, marked *sf,* with a line. Then they leap to another quarter-note which, though a seventh higher, is actually a resolution of the accented chord; but this resolution is marked simply *mf,* also with a line. Obviously the line added to the accent indicates the duration factor. The title of the movement shows that the flute timbre is to be emphasized, and besides, the sudden minor chord could well call for expressive inflection. The volume issue is not too clear; the flutes enter *piano,* in the second bar they make a *crescendo* to *mf,* and in the third bar a *diminuendo,* but how far is not indicated. However, for the resolution chord to sound no stronger than the accented chord, the latter must be played more loudly, as it lies in a weaker register of the flutes than the resolution chord; consequently there must be a volume factor in the accent. An acute attack, though, is not necessary and would be out of character. Therefore, the accent type is 26.

In the second bar of the "Waltz of the Flowers," the half-note is accented with both symbols *sf* and >, in *forte!* *(Fig. 71)* It looks as if the composer meant this one to be a whopper; but he has added no power instruments to reinforce his woodwinds and horns, which any composer, certainly he of all, would have done were that his intention. So let us inquire as to what he could have meant. There are lines over all the surrounding quarter-notes; so duration and breadth of tone are already in the picture. It would be contrary to all artistic logic to suppose that those factors are to be omitted from the culminating note of the phrase. This leaves the acute and volume factors still to be considered; and while the double accent marking is curious and highly personal, there may be "method in it." The most plausible explanation is that Chaikovsky felt that one of his two accent marks merely incorporated the lines with which the other notes are marked, and the other accent mark gave the note something extra; in this case, the extra something would much more appropriately be a factor of volume than of acuteness; so let us select type 26 for this accent. The whole theme gets going in bar 38, and the chord corresponding to the first accented one occurs in bar 39; but here the accent type should be not 26 but 23, particularly because the whole theme is marked *dolce cantabile.*

We may have a specimen of the rare type 9 in the last bar of the first ending of the first repeated strain. *(Fig. 72)* This is an eighth-note, on which some instruments enter to reinforce it, at the end of a *crescendo* which began in *forte;* the next eighth-note is the first of a *legato* scale of five eighth-notes which leads into the next melody note. So the dynamic level of the accented note is at least *ff,* and it must be cut very short so that the ensuing scale will come out clearly. And an acute attack is unquestionably needed here as well.

The accent in the third bar of the second ending is somewhat similar, except that the need for shortening the accented note is not as great, since there is an eighth-rest after it. *(Fig. 73)* Accordingly, if this accent does not include the shortening factor, it is an example of the rare type 1 or 2—probably the latter, as the following music is *ff.*

Thus far Chaikovsky is shown to have been quite rational in his use of accents, at least in a typical example of his successful "light" music. We have come to no conclusion yet as to whether he made any distinction between what he meant by the different symbols he used, though we have seen that, usually unnecessarily, he helps the interpreter out with explicit guides. Perhaps an inquiry into his *Pathetic Symphony,* probably his greatest gift to posterity, will shed more light on the subject. For the instrumentation of the opening of his symphony, he chose all the most imperfect and reedy-sounding instruments of the orchestra: the violas and double-basses (the two modern survivors of the viol family) and a lone bassoon. Firm-sounding instruments such as celli or brass are avoided. The bassoon announces the theme in a three-bar sequence, the first bar *pp,* the second *p,* the third *mp.* Its uniform rhythmic pattern comprises an upbeat of two rising eighth-notes, the next higher note for a quarter's value, then a half-note on the next note below. The fourth member of the sequence is taken over by half of the violas, *mf, crescendo,* upbow, who play the same motive that the bassoon had with the difference that what had been the quarter-note is now a half-note, downbow; and this half-note bears a *sf,* as do the bassoon, the other half of the violas, and all the basses on their note, which is a whole-note. All the parts are marked *diminuendo* to *piano. (Fig. 74)*

Some conductors conceive this accent as a violent one, directing the strings to begin their downbow *before* changing their wrists from the upbow position to the downbow position, thus producing an acute attack. While Chaikovsky's poetic content often requires explosive accents, it may be questioned whether we have progressed enough into this large work, which gets into its stride at considerable leisure, to take such an intense interpretation of this accent. At any rate, the score indicates a steady *crescendo* from the beginning, and thus calls for a volume factor; and the timbres chosen are certainly deliberate and should be emphasized, as well as the mounting expressive intensity of the sequential theme; so the accent type will be either 16 or 25. The latter seems preferable by the additional fact that from the answering entrance of the oboes to the end of the introduction the notes corresponding to the previously accented one are not accented, but simply *mf.*

The *allegro* begins with a theme based on the bassoon theme of the introduction. The strings have it for four bars, of which the last two are in sixteenth-notes, then the flutes and clarinets take it up. *(Fig. 75)* When the sixteenth-note passage is reached by the woodwinds, the first flute part has accents, marked >, on the first note of each of three of the groups of four sixteenth-notes. These accented notes are all slurred to their successors, which in the first two instances are a sixth below, and in the last, a half step below. The dynamics are *piano.* The skip of a sixth, in the major mode, gives a touch of wistful light to what had previously been, in the strings, a simple stepwise droop, in the minor mode; and this point is one of the important data in the analysis of the accent. An acute factor, in addition to the difference in pitch of the following note, would produce a disproportionate disparity between the character of the accented note and that of its successor, in at least the first two instances, so that the melodic line would thereby be distorted. Hence it should not be present; nor, by the same token, should a volume factor. But an expressive color, merged with the limpid timbre of the flute, is decidedly in order. As to the lengthening factor, the fact that the accented notes are slurred to their successors would, as a rule, preclude any extension of their correct duration. However, here we have a rare case in which an exception should be made, and the lengthening factor should be present nevertheless—to effect a lingering, if ever so slight, on the accented notes, for purely expressive purposes. It will necessarily bring in the note after each accented note a hairsbreadth late. A further profusion of words here would serve our purposes far less than one performance of the passage in the manner outlined, with accents of type 23.

Before the appearance of the second main subject, there is a long transitional passage, after several pages of which the direction *"Un poco animando"* appears. The horns enter in the bar following this direction, marked *f,* on inner voices among the trumpets and trombones, also marked *f,* and below all the woodwinds except the bassoons, marked *ff.* The first and third horns and first bassoon have three eighth-notes of an inner voice all to themselves, all three of which bear accents denoted by the symbol >. *(Fig. 76)* Chaikovsky must have known that without some help this voice would never be actually heard among the surrounding amount of sound. Besides, it consists of the neighboring tone above the correct harmony note, then the neighboring tone below it, and finally the correct harmony note itself, so it is an important expressive voice. For all these reasons, acoustical as well as expressive, these accents should have the factors of acuteness, volume, tone quality, and lengthening, and hence be of type 17.

A few bars farther on there is a direction *"Un poco piu animato."* In the third and fourth bars, counting from this direction, there are accents marked > in the sustaining parts, on the quarter-notes beginning on the first and third beats of the bars. *(Fig. 77)* The dynamics are *ff,* and the leading voices, which are not accented, enter one sixteenth's value after each accented tone. The accented tones are all slurred to their successors, voices in chords to which the accented chords resolve; and the successors are all eighth-notes. Obviously the accented chords are intended to have both weight and impact; and the chords to which they resolve must have something less, though still in *fortissimo.* The effect can be realized with accents of type 16, with a slight *diminuendo* into each resolution chord, and care being taken that the resolution chords also be fully audible.

The development section, recapitulation, and coda of this mighty movement are full of instances that show clearly that the composer made no distinction whatever in his mind or practice between the meaning of the different accent symbols, with these two minor exceptions: that like Mendelssohn but unlike Beethoven, he is reluctant to use the symbol *sf* (1) on two or more successive notes that follow close together, and (2) when the dynamics are *p* or softer. But we can be sure that as to the type of accent called for, the symbols are identical.

It will not profit us to examine the remainder of the accents in this symphony in detail. Enough has been set forth for us to be certain that in his accents Chaikovsky, highly personal though his form and content be, is nonetheless fully comprehensible and accessible according to the laws of musical truth as exemplified in the works of the classic masters.

NINE

STRAUSS AND DEBUSSY

Strauss and Debussy have little in common other than being contemporaries, and each of them having put virtually all his eggs in one basket. For his value, the one depends on the listener's direct enjoyment of the melodies he spins, the stunning harmonic progressions, the glittering orchestration, the ingenious and viable counterpoint, the towering edifices of tone as things in themselves. All these elements, together with the characters of the various passages, are calculated to afford the listener purely sensuous pleasure, often the pleasure of experiencing ugliness, but in any case it goes straight from the ear to the brain and/or the heart. With the other, melody, harmony, counterpoint, and orchestration never serve as ends in themselves, as physical phenomena to be observed and savored; they are of use to the composer solely as means of conjuring up images, atmospheres, or states of consciousness to the hearer, and sometimes of even wafting him into a pleasant and aimless reverie.

The one fascinated his hearers, as well as himself, with the beauty and intricacy of the machinery he contrived: the acceptance of his music rests largely on our appreciation of the machinery, as it is paraded for our admiration; indeed it is almost as attractive while at rest as when running. The other begins to reach us only when we cease to be aware of the machinery. The one succeeds to the extent that he is granted bright light and alert attention, and he invariably loses when the hearer's attention is allowed to falter; to the other, clear light and energetic listening are fatal, since he is interested only in casting spells. Had they both been painters, the one would have been a prodigal consumer of pigment, sweeping it on into vast colorful spectacles crammed with significant (and insignificant) detail—a Rubens, a David, a Delacroix; the other would have been a delicate dabber of half tints whose pictures assume form and meaning only when one steps away to a certain distance from them, whence one can no longer distinguish the lines and brush-strokes—a Seurat, a Whistler, a Monet. The one worked with materials, and in styles, previously developed and established; the other truly invented his own style and basic individual procedures. In their successes they are both among the supreme magicians of the realm of tone; but their failures would have been less abysmal had each less rigorously excluded from his own music all the qualities of the other.

Yet with all the diametrical conflict in their aesthetics, their uses of accents are equally open to analysis along the lines hitherto indicated in this survey. Let us look first at one of Strauss' masterpieces, if not his outstanding success, the tone poem *Till Eulenspiegel's Merry Pranks.* The work begins with a tranquil statement, in the strings, of one of the two principal themes. *(Fig. 78)* In the second bar two clarinets and bassoons enter, doubling the chord of the strings; and these woodwind parts are marked *sfzp,* while the strings are marked *p.* The clarinets' note is sustained for three eighths, while the bassoons' is a dotted eighth followed by two sixteenths which are higher tones of the same chord. In the fifth bar the clarinets are alone on high C and A, the dynamics being less than *piano,* and they are joined in the second half of the bar by two flutes, which enter on the F and C next below the clarinets. All four of these parts are held over to the beginning of the next bar. The flute entrance is also marked *sfzp*.

Strauss uses the symbols interchangeably, except that, like Mendelssohn and Chaikovsky, he shrinks from putting two or more *sf*'s in close succession. He uses both symbols when the context is both loud and soft, on long notes and short, and on notes which are detached as well as slurred to their predecessors. Accordingly we shall disregard the kind of symbol in discussing the interpretation of these accents. Till Eulenspiegel was a slippery rogue, and naturally the composer must have intended to portray his nature right from the beginning. Hindsight shows us that his purpose in the first accent was to supplement the dry tone of the strings with (1) the oily sound of the clarinets' holding-notes and (2) the mischievous sound of the bassoons, shortly followed by the sneaking effect of their movement. This reasoning shows us that the tone color should be a factor in the accent. The strings move flowingly, so that an acute attack in the woodwinds would be inappropriate. The duration factor cannot be involved, but the volume factor seems called for by the indications that the composer wanted the woodwind entrance clearly heard—the significance of which we shall perceive when we discuss the epilogue of the work. Therefore the accent type is 25, with the volume factor evaporating quickly.

The sign *p* along with the *sfz* ordinarily gives rise to quite an ambiguity, because of the following possibilities: (1) the prevailing dynamic level is *piano*. Then either (a) the accent is in *piano* and the *p* is superfluous, or (b) the accent is intended to be in a dynamic level of its own, higher than *piano,* followed by a return to *piano* at the expiration of the accent. On the other hand, if (2) the prevailing dynamic level is higher than *piano,* (a) it becomes reduced to *piano* with and on the accent (the accent thus being in *piano*), or (b) the accent is in the prevailing dynamic level, and the reduction to *piano* takes place on the accented note but not before the expiration of the accent. With all the alternatives thus before us, the one we should choose as the most fitting in this instance is 1(a). The musical context would be contradicted by any other choice.

The fifth bar accent in the flutes occurs on a unique orchestral effect. How could anyone but Strauss have conceived a flute entrance as pro

viding a rhythmical pulse? That this is indeed the effect can be understood by imagining this bar with the flutes omitted and nothing sub-
stituted for them. The entrance not only keeps the movement alive but
also, with its cold interval of a fourth, provides a "dead-pan" mood of
expectancy, which is promptly satisfied by the appearance, in the next
bar, of the wonderful and notorious horn solo theme. For the rhythmical function of the flute entrance, the accent needs the acute factor. It
also needs the limpid sound of the flutes; but because of the softness of
the clarinets, a volume factor would be too much, so this accent is
type 13.

The horn solo theme, the pride and nemesis of all hornists, so successfully belies the ingenious craftsmanship in which it was fashioned
that it has become one of the most familiar and seemingly inevitable
musical ideas in the entire literature. (*Fig. 79*) This has come about
despite its impish characterization on the most unimpish instrument in
the orchestra, and despite the fact that its rhythmical displacements
never "come off," because of the lack of any steady rhythmic reference
anywhere else in the orchestra; and also because its first note that falls
on a strong beat is a passing tone to another passing tone, and thus is
one which the unaided ear would be least likely to select as coinciding
with a strong beat. But its universally satisfying effect is due partly to
precisely this idiosyncrasy, partly to its infectious melodic line, and
partly to its felicitous allocation to the horn—inasmuch as it contains
only one note, occurring three times, that fails to conform exactly to the
range, playable notes, and in a liberal sense the style, of the natural valve-
less horn. It is a seven-bar theme, in 6/8 time, and its initial motive, literally repeated three times, extends over seven eighth-notes, so that it
occupies a different position in the bar each time! And it comes out
right—that is, with its naturally stressed notes coinciding with the
strong beats—only the last time. Of the two quarter-notes in the motive,
which are next to each other, the first now falls on the bar-line. Both
it and its successor are marked >, the third time only.

To reassure the hearer that the rhythm is now set "right," and to
point up the syncopation of the second quarter-note, these accents
should have the acute factor. As to color, there is no more reason for
either the horn timbre or expressive intensity on these two notes than

anywhere else in the theme. And since a *crescendo* is marked in the middle of the following bar, a volume increase is not intended here. But a lengthening factor definitely is indicated—not only because in the first two occurrences of the motive these two notes were slurred together, showing that full length belongs to the notes; nor even solely because the second of these two notes now has a second eighth-note's value which it lacked previously, but for both these reasons plus the main reason, which is that the theme is nearing its climax, and there must be no slack in the tension of its progress that would "allow the ball to drop" and so vitiate the cumulative excitement that has been building up quickly since its beginning. Hence the accents should be of type 8.

As to the next two accents, on the low C and F (concert pitch), let us observe that the theme really ends on the F just before, and these last two notes merely drive the theme home. But they furnish an important home-driving nonetheless, and the player should "sit down" on each note. As in the two previous accents, there is plenty of reason for an acute attack and a lengthening factor; here also a volume factor would be in order, by way of implementing the *crescendo* in the bar before, so these accents are of type 11.

After a complete restatement of the horn theme, part of it is cackled by the oboes, and then by the clarinets, continually under a tremolo in the violins. *(Fig. 79)* The last note of both the oboes and clarinets, the seventh of a dominant seventh chord, is reinforced by several other wind instruments, all of which hold the tone for nearly two entire bars. This note—in both cases beginning on the second eighth of the bar, and in *forte*—is marked *sfz;* and at the same point the strings, whose dynamics up to there are *piano,* are also marked *sfz,* with *dim.* added.

As before with the horn, all sense of bar-lines is lost, so much so that the last long note of both the oboes and the clarinets always sounds as if it were the first eighth of the bar, instead of the second. From the lack of any attempt on the composer's part to counteract this, it is certain that he was satisfied with it. The long note, then, must surely have an acute attack; and considering its extreme length, it must have been intended to bawl insistently, and thus some expressive color is needed. The lengthening factor is not vital here, as, say, a sixty-fourth's value in such a long note would be negligible; but since the inordinate length of the tone is an important element of its expression, this full length should be given it, and its importance emphasized to the players. Lastly, a volume factor, but only at the tone's inception, should impart to it the needed impact; therefore our accent type is 17. When we look at the violin parts, we see from the *"dim."* that follows the *sfz* that a volume factor is intended. It should be that and no more, or the composer would have written in a higher dynamic level to so indicate; but the *diminuendo* from it must be spread over the entire remainder of the bar, for the *"dim."* is placed at the end of the bar, and it is followed by a *"cresc."* This calls for an unusual accent, being spread out over several notes. The first one should have an acute attack, plus, as has been said, a volume factor, the type thus being 2; the others should have only the volume factor and be of type 5.

No further accents in this score require comment before Number 16. In the seventh and eighth bars after 16, the clarinets have, in *piano,* accents on grace notes on the same pitch as the principal notes, and the whole two-bar phrase has one slur over it. The trumpets double the clarinets' line, also slurred, and have the accents, but on the principal notes, as the grace notes are lacking; while the violas and celli also double the line, with the grace notes but without both the slur and the accents. So do the second violins, in *pizzicato* chords, without grace notes. *(Fig. 80)*

Let us see, first, what the effect of the slur can be. Does it tie any of the grace notes to their principal notes, thus bringing about a mere anticipation of the principal notes? It might, if it were not for the fact that the accepted notation for such an effect always requires a small or "local" slur just from the grace note to its principal note. Hence we must conclude that, since there is no such small slur here, the general slur over the whole phrase is not sufficiently specific as to tie the grace note to its principal note. What, then, does the slur do? Let us reason thus: if the grace notes were not there, but the slur were, all the notes in the phrase would be tied together, *legato.* If the slur were not there, but the grace notes were, all the notes in the phrase would be detached from one another. Now since the grace notes and their principal notes, as we have seen, cannot be tied together, the only effect that the slur can possibly have is to tie together the only remaining notes, *viz.,* each principal note with the grace note *after* it.

Having disposed of this question, we can now address ourselves to the accents. As we have just reasoned, the accented notes are approached by slur, so there can be no question of an acute attack. The accented notes are too short to allow of the application of expressive or instrumental color, and the duration question is already precluded by the rule that grace notes must have the shortest possible value. Accordingly the volume factor is left as the only one available for effectuating the accent; and the type is 5. The trumpets, however, having the accents on the principal notes, have time to apply color also, to which the music lends itself; hence their accents should be of type 25.

Simultaneous with these accents there is another unusual one in the horns and bassoons. These instruments hold one chord over two bars; and on their notes of the second bar (the same as of the first, and tied over) there is an accent. The chord is a dominant seventh, and it resolves to the tonic, except for the horns, which evaporate; and most of the orchestra has a *crescendo* marked in the bar of the horns' and bassoons' accent. While these data do not necessarily indicate that the accent should take the form of a *crescendo,* it certainly indicates that the accented notes must at least be fully sustained, and with vitality, for their full value. Thus we have the color and lengthening factors. The attack cannot possibly be an acute one. The volume factor seems well in order, and here one can reasonably argue as to whether it must appear at the bar-line or afterward, as *crescendo.* Our conclusion, then, is for an accent of type 26 or 37. This discussion will be found applicable to many situations in the passage following this point. Its climax is reached with the pause on the F of the horns, five bars before Number 20. This F is the last note of an altered version of the first bar of the original horn theme, in the four horns in unison and alone; and each of the first four notes of it (in the preceding bar) is accented. The dynamics are *fff. (Fig. 81)*

This call of the horns must continue the tension of the preceding passage, which has worked up to a *fortissimo* of the whole orchestra; and thus the volume and color factors are indicated. It must be "punched out" and hence have also the acute factor. But since (1) the notes are detached, (2) there are four instruments playing in unison, not just one or two, and (3) the instruments are horns, which are the most sluggish-speaking instruments of the orchestra, each accented note should be made quite short in the interests of both character and clarity—involving the shortening factor. Therefore these accents should be of type 18.

Let us now skip over to the epilogue—so named in the score, and anyway recognizable as such by being almost identical, for a while, with the very opening of the work. The clarinets and bassoons enter, exactly as before, but with this notable difference, that in the epilogue they are *not* accented! In that one accent, which was present at the beginning but is not now, is concentrated the entire difference between the portrayal of Till in life and the retrospect of him in death! And with this inconspicuous but eloquent instance we can fittingly close our brief observation of the significance of accents in the aesthetics of the master Richard Strauss.

If Debussy's use of accents differs in any way from Strauss'—or Mozart's—it is solely because the different character of his music calls for other aspects of accent interpretation, though according to principles in no wise different from those we have been outlining. Take, for example, the first accent in his *L'Après-Midi d'un Faune*. The whole work is a dream picture of a motionless, steaming afternoon in a far-away forest that never existed. It begins with the sound of the faun piping nonchalantly on his flute; as he pauses for breath, oboes, clarinets, and harp softly breathe a half-diminished seventh chord. *(Fig. 82)* One eighth-beat later a horn adds its tone to the E in the chord, sustaining it for three slow eighths and repeating it for two more, before it leads the ensemble into the chord of resolution in the next bar. It is not needed for spelling out the harmony; its only possible purposes are to furnish a melodic line and to heighten expression and atmosphere. It seems to add a note of longing, perhaps of nameless uneasiness, to the whole picture. Anyway, it must sing subtly and express exquisitely—especially as its first note is accented. An acute attack would surely trouble the mythical tranquillity. A lengthening factor is not involved since the accented note is tied to its successor. But color certainly is called for, plenty of it. As for volume, there is no need for such except a slight *crescendo-diminuendo* to maintain the horn's audibility through the *crescendo-diminuendo* of the harp. So we have here an accent of pure color, applied at the tone's inception, plus a volume factor applied later; and this gives us a class E combination of types 22 and 30.

Oddly enough, while this work was written for, and first performed by, a Paris orchestra, the horns used in the Paris orchestras are incapable of producing the poetical effects possible with the German type horns in general use practically everywhere else. The Parisian horns are built with entirely different proportions from the German type, and produce a tone that is quite "open" and unmysterious, much like that of a saxophone. Furthermore, the Parisian hornists apply a vibrato—hardly any two players alike in number of cycles or amount of deviation from true pitch and average dynamics—which still further frustrates any possibility of magical faraway suggestions. All told, of all places in the world, Paris is the one in which the chances for the realization of Debussy's conception are the slimmest! Such are the ironies of art and life.

The next accent in this work that merits discussion is found at Number 3 where a new section begins, of a somewhat agitated character. A clarinet enters *piano crescendo* on the upbeat, reaches *forte* on the bar-line, and diminishes, returning to *piano* on the third quarter. *(Fig. 83)*

The third horn, *piano,* shares the upbeat; then on the bar-line all four horns sound a chord, muted, and marked *sfz,* and then diminish along with the clarinet. The most challenging question in this accent concerns the volume factor. There are two difficulties: the mutes, and the absence of a dynamic mark on the horn chord.

As to the former, there is ordinarily an ambiguity where a dynamic mark or accent is applied to a muted instrument. A mute not only lessens the volume of a tone, but also pinches the timbre; so that a given amount of force exerted by the player on a muted instrument will produce a weaker and thinner sound than on the same instrument unmuted. The ambiguity lies in the question of whether the mark refers to the sound that issues, or to the force exerted by the player.

Here it is obvious that the four horns must constitute a homogeneous choir, all sounding alike. But they must also maintain a certain relationship with the clarinet, which, in *forte* (and, of course, unmuted), carries the highest voice of the chord. Now an unmuted horn, *forte,* is stronger than a clarinet, *forte;* but a muted horn, *forte,* is approximately equal to a clarinet, *forte;* and a muted horn, *piano,* is much weaker than a clarinet, *forte;* but if accented, and with a volume factor, it would be heard almost as strongly as the clarinet. Since the clarinet, while still the leading voice, soon dips below the topmost horn, it is clear that it should be stronger than that horn, and as the horns are all equal, stronger than any of the horns. Evidently, then, the last-mentioned alternative is the one the composer intended. The *p* on the third horn's upbeat applies to all horns, and it refers to the sound they produce, not the force exerted by the players, which should be considerably more than *piano*. The volume factor superimposed on this *piano* should decline gradually to keep pace with the clarinet's *diminuendo*.

As for the other factors, an acute attack is called for, because of (1) the suddenness of the effect of the horn chord, harmonywise as well as timbrewise, (2) the agitated character of the new section, and (3) the players' necessity to tongue smartly in order to make their instruments "speak" clearly on the beat through the mutes. As timbre is part of the effect, the color factor is also required; but since the accented chord is tied to its successor, duration is not involved. The type, then, is 16.

A peculiar situation confronts us in the next bar, in which the celli and basses, *piano* and unmuted, have one eighth note, *pizzicato,* on the second quarter, marked $>$, and the celli and other strings have a double stop, *pizzicato,* on the third quarter, marked *sfz*. *(Fig. 84)* On its face this looks like an intended difference of force or quality between the two; and in fact this passage is often so performed. However, such an interpretation is erroneous. The clarinet, which is the only other instrument playing at the spot of the *sfz* chord, has difficulty being heard if all the strings except the basses play *forte,* even though the clarinet's note coincides with the topmost note of the strings. For both of these accented notes to conform to the prevailing mood of the passage—which can be described as "slight agitation within pastoral languor"—it will be correct, and ample, to have them plucked smartly with the merest increase over the dynamic level of *piano,* both to produce equal volume, except that the larger number of strings sounded in the second one will naturally yield a louder sound. This gives us an accent of type 2; or if the strings are left to *"laisser vibrer"* a bit, it will be 4.

After Number 8, there is a double bar, marked *Un peu plus animé.* In this bar the oboe rather tartly answers the lovely and gentle flute solo with a brusque rejoinder *(Fig. 85),* which Shera * considers a fleeting vision of nymphs. He must consider nymphs to be rather nasty creatures, for it is hard to see how the oboe's figure, in the instrument's low register, could characterize graceful feminine allure, nor is its support, consisting of a slow tremolo on the muted horns, evocative of anything particularly enchanting. This interpretation is borne out by the *sfz* with a *diminuendo* on the oboe's second note, which, like its first note, is low G, but with a trill attached to it. Moreover, there is no direction of *"doux"* such as there is accompanying several other passages in the score elsewhere. If one were to illustrate this passage with visual images, one could best do so with an entrance of goblins, toads, insects, and other such unwelcome folk, always, however, still seen through, and softened by, the shimmer of a legendary summer haze. To complete the orchestral picture, on the last quarter clarinets and bassoons take over the horns' figure, while the strings pluck the chord, *pp* with an accent. The bar is then repeated literally.

The oboe's accent, because of the *diminuendo,* was conceived as including the volume factor; and curiously enough, since the accent is on a trill, the auxiliary note also takes some of the accent. Debussy evidently wanted a piquant touch, a faint sting, in this bar and its repetition, judging from the two accents, one of which, significantly, is on a *pizzicato* note; hence let us include a "bite" in the oboe accent (only on the first note, of course, the G, as the A's in the trill are necessarily all slurred). The deftness of Debussy's orchestration permits of no doubt that here the oboe's timbre is an important element of the expression, and therefore the color factor is also called for. As for duration, let us observe that the next note is a grace note, and the accented note is not slurred to it; therefore for this grace note to be successfully articulated a slight shortening of the accented note will be advisable.

* In *Debussy ana Ravel* in the Oxford Press "The Musical Pilgrim" series, at p. 26.

Thus the accent type is 18. Six bars later the same music reappears, with the English horn now taking the oboe's part, and the oboe transferred to the previous flute solo. The accent type should be the same, the reasoning therefore being corroborated by the timbre effect of the oboe and English horn.

L'Après-Midi d'un Faune, with all its gossamer haze, is nonetheless near the extreme degree to which program music can go. The picture it describes is a definite and concrete one. While the allusion of any detail is open to question, all the details taken together with relation to one another and the whole can make sense only by reference to the one intended specific impression. And the picture is a miniature, as will be clearly realized when one compares it to *La Mer.* The sea, with its vast expanse and limitless moods, cannot be conceived except on a large scale. And details of marine scenery, at rest and in motion, lend themselves to representation in music with a higher degree of certainty and accuracy than most of the details (if there are any) in *L'Après-Midi d'un Faune.* Knowing *La Mer* to have been written twelve years after *L'Après-Midi,* one would have reason to expect it to be a mighty and vivid portrayal in tone of salient aspects of the great waters that cover most of the earth. We find it to be nothing of the kind. Debussy renounced his great opportunity to paint; or perhaps he was no longer capable of painting. In fact, he even does the reverse; for in *L'Après-Midi* one can be more certain of the identity of each image suggested in the music, than one can in *La Mer.*

Surely one reason for this is that in the intervening twelve years Debussy, like so many other creators of art, had written out much of his stock of original ideas and had begun to use, in place of the consumed ones, a more complex elaboration of his remaining and attenuating material. The richest vein of the mine had been largely exhausted, leaving only lower grade ore, which always requires more intensive treatment to be fashioned into something of equal value. Along with this process, in Debussy as well as many others, went a partial withdrawal from worldly life and interest, and an intensification of his personal inner life, and of his probings into the ultimate secrets of art. The things they created took on a highly subjective cast, expressing their private urges relatively more, and the realities of the world around them relatively less. In this phase, also, the tools of the trade take on larger significance than that of mere means to an end—they tend to develop into substantial realities, objects of interest and importance in themselves.

Accordingly in *La Mer* we find more of Mr. Debussy, strange and sophisticated virtuoso poet in tones, than we do of green salt water. And if the titles of the three movements of the work were scrambled so that each one were affixed to a movement other than its proper one, virtually no injustice would be done to the music; for even if the titles compassed a wide range of moods, which they do not, there would be about an equal amount of music in each movement to correspond to each. Well might it be said of this work, as Beethoven wrote at the head of his own *Pastoral Symphony,* "Mehr Ausdruck der Empfindung als Malerei"—"the expression of feeling, rather than painting."

There are a great many accents in the work, and as usual we shall not attempt to discuss more than a picked few of them. The first few pages of the score are the only ones in the entire work which might more aptly fit the title of the movement in which they are found than that of either of the other movements. They could well suggest the sea before, and then as, the sun rises. After five dark and calm bars, the violins enter, *pp,* in octaves on high B's, *tremolando. (Fig. 86)* In their second bar of the same they increase to *p* in the third bar, and then descend slowly and exit. Then a principal theme is announced, after which the violins make their second entrance, similar to the first in all respects except that the note is marked with a line and the symbol >; also the *crescendo* is in the first bar, and the descent starts in the second bar, so that the two bars of the violins' first entrance are now compressed to one. The remainder of the orchestra is the same both times, except that the timpani and basses play B the first time and D the second, and the interior motive is slightly more fully orchestrated the second time. This second entrance plainly suggests the dawn in a more advanced stage than the first, and hence it should be of an amplitude greater in some degree and/or quality, which the accent will serve to make it.

Since all indications point to this accent's being one of color rather than impact, it should be a plain one. Color is certainly called for, since the passage is as much one of pure nature-suggestion as any in the whole work, and Debussy chose his orchestration carefully. Care should be taken to keep the first violins very quiet and to bring out the seconds slightly, so that both notes of the octave will be heard in equal strength. The volume factor, too, should be present; but should it be on only the first stroke of the tremolo or extend into two or more strokes? This question must be asked because of the line over the note in addition to the accent, which indicates an intention of the composer to have the application of the accent extend beyond the instant of entrance. But it is still uncertain whether this duration factor involves a lengthening of the very first stroke of the tremolo, and this question can best be left to the conductor's taste. Thus this accent is of type 26.

Let us now examine the accents in the celebrated passage for the cello section, beginning two bars before Number 9. *(Fig. 87)* The time signature is four-four; the celli are divided into four parts, with two instruments on each part in the first two bars, and *four* on each part (no unemployment here!) thereafter. The dynamics begin *piano,* following a long *diminuendo* down to complete silence; on the first quarter there is a *crescendo,* marked upbow, and on the second, a *sfz p* $>$ with downbow and a line, the basses joining in with a quarter-note, *pizzicato, sfz* (otherwise unmarked), while the timpani begin a roll, marked *sfz pp* $<$ *p* $>$. On the eighth-note after the second quarter the four horns enter, *sfz* $>$, on the same notes as those played by the celli—and in the next bar their mark is *pp* $<$ $>$ on the same chord, still tied over.

Obviously in this accent something less than the maximum power is conceived, or else the full complement of celli, instead of only half thereof, would have been used. Furthermore, the maximum power, even of just the instruments that are playing, would not be called for with the dynamics starting at, and quickly returning to, *piano.* Estimating the amount of *crescendo* at its reasonable limit, it would take the *p* up two stages to *mf;* and the accent superimposed on that, if it be deemed to include a volume factor, would raise it to no more than *f.* And since the dynamic nuance is part of the expression here, the volume factor should be present. The percussive effect of the timpani and basses indicate a smart attack, an acute factor. The timbre of the eight celli is also an essential element and together with the line over the accented note indicates the need of the color factor. Thus for the celli, the accent type is 17, the lengthening factor, however, affecting only the color, which should persist to the end of the tone in the next bar; the volume factor must expire very quickly, and the sound of the celli must gradually fade away from *piano* to silence over a period of six quarters.

The dynamics of the celli have to be extended to the basses, for it would not make sense to have the basses operating under their last dynamics mark, of the previous bar, which is *ppp*. While some composers, such as Sibelius, have a habit of writing *pizzicato* half-notes, dotted half-notes and even whole-notes, Debussy rarely writes a note longer than a quarter-note to be played *pizzicato,* a quarter being almost the longest *pizzicato* note in his vocabulary. Here the basses have such a quarter note, so we must take it that it is intended to resound. Moreover, since there were many other instruments available and unused for supplying that note, which is the root of the chord, we must assume that the bass color was desired. Finally, the accompanying orchestration clearly indicates an acute factor—so this accent is of type 17 also. As for the timpani, we observe that all the choirs playing here have their *crescendi* and *diminuendi* at different times, so that the combination of sounds from instant to instant is quite an acoustic effect. The timpani participate very prominently in this effect, as they make a *crescendo* while all the other instruments are making a *diminuendo;* but on the initial accent their tone must of course be adjusted to balance with the celli as to volume, tone color, and duration. The striking entrance of the horns needs but the acute and color factors. All the needed volume will be forthcoming without requiring any of it from the accent. The horns' accent type is 13.

Several of the accents in this movement are of the ∧ kind, which is discussed in the Appendix. And the second movement presents no problems that need detain us. In the third movement, however, there are some matters that require comment. In its ninth bar, at Number 43, over a sudden *pp* roll on the timpani and tremolo in the basses, *ponticello,* the oboes and clarinets enter with a large seventh chord.

(Fig. 88) While the clarinets hold their tones into the third bar, the trumpets enter in unison with them, muted, but sustain for only a quarter and an eighth. On the third quarter of the second bar, the oboes, maintaining their interval of a major third, descend a half-tone, which they hold over the second bar-line; then they descend another half-tone, rise again a half-tone, and then another to regain their original notes. As they do so, the trumpets reenter as before, and the clarinets attack the same notes again, sustaining through the next bar. Both times the trumpets are marked *mf* > with a line, and *diminuendo*. The oboes and clarinets, on their entrance, are marked *sfz>p*, then *diminuendo,* and *crescendo* up to the return of the original notes, which is marked *sfz* with a *diminuendo* to *p* on the next bar-line, plus a further *diminuendo* throughout the next bar. The timpani have a *crescendo* from *pp* throughout the first and third bars, and a *diminuendo* throughout the second and fourth, so that twice they are in the middle of a *crescendo* while the woodwinds are making a *diminuendo*. The gong, too, is struck, *p,* on the woodwind entrance and at the spot at which the original note returns.

After five bars of the introductory motive of agitated expectancy, the same theme reappears as at Number 43, but in a higher key and with the woodwinds doubled by the four horns, muted, an octave below, and the trumpets being silent. This time all the winds enter *p* with a line, and make a steady *crescendo* up to the instant of the return to the initial notes. This *crescendo* is marked *mf* at the bar-line of the third bar; and the initial note's return is marked *sfz diminuendo* in all parts, while the woodwinds have a >, and a line on the note besides. The gong is also heard at the same points as before, but now marked *p* >. As the next bar is *pp*, the *diminuendo* must be rapid.

Let us now look again at Number 43, the first appearance of the theme with which we are concerned. The first question that must be resolved is whether the > mark on the woodwind entrance is an accent or a *diminuendo*. If one examines other comparable markings throughout the score, one notices many instances of a > immediately following a *f, ff,* or *sfz,* sometimes followed by a *p* or *pp,* between the staves, and not as near to any note as it could have been printed. These marks are clearly *diminuendi*. Many other appearances of the symbol are directly above or below a note, several in *crescendo* passages. In such places the symbol cannot mean a *diminuendo,* and can mean only an accent. Such comparison assures us that what the symbol means here is a *diminuendo* in the woodwinds and an accent in the trumpets; so that all parts enter with an accent (in the woodwinds symbolized by *sfz*).

Now to analyze the accent, the question of the acute factor is a close one. While the sustained and drooping contour of the theme and its thin orchestration would normally tend strongly to indicate a plain accent, the balance is swung in favor of an acute one here by (1) the agitated introduction leading up to it, and (2) the somewhat percussive entrance of the trumpets and gong, which not only constitutes evidence of the quality of the chord's leading edge, but also will somewhat cover the woodwinds if the latter do not assert themselves with an equivalent "bite." As the orchestration is decidedly coloristic, the color factor is also called for. The dramatic quality of the theme, and the orchestration as well, render unfitting a marked decrease in the instrumental color and the expressive tension; in fact, it would be hardly incorrect to say that the color and tension should be maintained throughout the theme. In this respect, then, the accent includes also the lengthening factor. As to the volume factor, it must be pointed out that the players are required to drop to *piano* in the space of no more than a fast quarter-note, and continue being heard; if they enter *fortissimo,* that result is both technically and acoustically difficult. The best they can do within reason is to drop from *f* to *p*. So let us impute a dynamics mark of *mf* which, together with a volume factor in the accent, will produce a *f* entrance of the woodwinds.

In the trumpets, the color interest should also be sustained to the end, even though the tone has a *diminuendo*. The line on their notes lends weight to this conclusion. The first and second accents of all the winds are alike, the type being 17.

The next entrance of the theme follows a brusque *pizzicato* note in the lower strings, which in effect compensates for the accent at number 43 which is omitted here. This entrance contains but one accent, at the spot where the original notes return. In the woodwind it is marked *sfz* with a line and a > above the note, while the horns have only the *sfz*. On the same beat the strings repeat the *pizzicato* note. The markings of the woodwinds can be interpreted only as a double accent, that is, one imparting to the tone a double portion of accented quality more than it would have if unaccented—a wise direction, to enable the woodwinds to hold their own against the horns. Their accent will again be of type 17, in double quantity, while that of the horns will also be 17 (single), and as to all, the volume factor will terminate considerably before the color. The gong marking (*p* $\diagdown$) is most perplexing. Coming on the intensified repetition of the theme as it does, a *diminuendo* cannot be forced into making sense—a gong always naturally makes a *diminuendo* anyway. However, if we consider the *diminuendo* symbol as an accent gone slightly awry, it all makes perfect sense, as a type 17 accent.

Nine bars after Number 52 a chorale-like theme appears, which had been heard before at the end of the first movement, and will be heard again at the end of the present one. *(Fig. 89)* In every one of its appearances the first four bars are identical (except that in the first one it begins in the major mode, and elsewhere, in the minor); the slight transformations that it undergoes occur only thereafter. Here it is in the key of E flat minor; it is in the horns, open, *piano;* there is a *crescendo* throughout the fourth bar, and the fifth and sixth bars are spanned by a dominant ninth on A flat, *subito pp* with a line. The theme then recommences—its seventh bar is at Number 53—with the *crescendo* now in the third bar of the recommencement, a *diminuendo* in the fourth, and a whole tone chord over the fifth and sixth, *p diminuendo* with an accent and a line. Both times, in the fifth bar, a trumpet enters *pp* with another motive consisting mainly of one sustained note; and two solo violins enter with a leisurely figuration, the first time on the bar-line, the second time after an eighth rest.

The surprising whole-tone chord is the salient feature of the accented spot. Whereas the chord at the corresponding spot six bars before had been softer than the sound immediately preceding it, here the chord is louder, for it is marked *p*—which is the volume level to which the sound had just returned after a *crescendo*—plus an accent and a line. And its effect is meant to take place right at its inception, for while the trumpet enters there, as before, the violins allow it an eighth's time

to establish itself without their intrusion. The theme is extremely tranquil, and there is nothing to call for an acute attack; but the volume
and color factors should certainly be present, the color being prolonged
as in the first accent in this movement—the type being 26.

The passage before Number 56 is one of heightening tension leading
into an expansive return of one of the themes, a completely linear one,
at Number 56. The initial motive of the theme consists of a triplet of
quarter-notes, the first two of which are the same, and the third of
which is a half-tone lower, and tied to a half-note which is further
tied over to another half-note in the next bar; then comes the same
triplet of quarter-notes again. *(Fig. 90)* The first two bars are repeated,
with the difference that the first note is a half-tone higher than before,
as is the second, but the third is the same as before, the descent to it
now being a whole-tone. The melodic line is given to the higher strings,
two horns, English horn, and piccolo. All of these have a slur extending over each pair of bars and a line on each note of the quarter-note
triplets; and in addition the horns and English horn have an accent on
each note of the quarter-note triplets. The orchestration is fairly full,
the dynamics *f,* with a *crescendo* throughout the second and fourth
bars.

An ambiguity arises in many instances where there is a slur over any
note and its immediate repetition. Such a combination is in many cases
properly performed as a single sustained tone; in others it is proper to
attack both notes separately. Since here the repeated notes are accented,
it is clear that they are not to be tied together, notwithstanding the
slur over the whole two-bar motive; and this judgment must also affect
the nonaccented voices as well. Significantly, in earlier appearances of
this theme, one instrument plays it *legato* while another, in unison with
it, has it detached; and at its first appearance it is marked *expressif et
soutenu*—so Debussy's intention clearly was for it to be sustained while
at the same time punctuated by the rhythm of all the notes! It seems
a clash of irreconcilable purposes, but it does "come off" when correctly executed.

The lowest octave of the theme is allocated to the accented instruments alone; the most reasonable inference from this fact is that it is
that octave which the composer considered the principal one, with the

higher instruments supplying an important but nonetheless secondary doubling; also, the accented instruments bear the burden of marking the separation of the quarter-notes, which is made still somewhat more onerous by the fact that in the doubling strings, the last two of each three quarter-notes are connected by a "local" slur. Even though that "local" slur is a direction for bowing rather than of phrasing, as such it could still cause a blurring of the separation of the notes, particularly in the *crescendo* at the end of the second and fourth bars. One more observation before considering the type of accent: all the instruments that play the melodic line, except the English horn and piccolo, are marked *très expressif*.

The line over the notes surely denotes a lengthening factor. Also, the horns' and English horn's need of maintaining their place in the tonal balance makes a volume factor most advisable. The whole setting, of which the direction *très expressif* is one of the minor elements, calls for tone intensity; and the above-mentioned need of clear articulation for the accented instruments (to say nothing of the others as well), would benefit by acute attacks on all the accented notes. The accent type, then, is 17. A good many of Beethoven's and Brahms' accents, as well as Debussy's, are also of this type—but observe the striking difference in the sounds produced by those accents in their various scores, due to the different contexts, styles, purposes and textures into which they are woven.

In summarizing Debussy's use of accents from the foregoing examples, one must acknowledge that it, like his harmonic system, form, and orchestration, was shaped by him so as to adequately convey the unprecedented content of his utterance. We observe in his case a greater reliance on accents, and a greater range in their functions, than with any of the other composers whose works we have examined. These features must be ascribed to the large part that specific, fleeting sounds, and details of timbre, play in his subject matter, not superficially for their sensory, ear-titillating effect, but for their legitimate usefulness in stimulating musico-emotional responses. He has his weaknesses, he shared many of his visions with us only in shapes spun out too thinly, and even at his greatest, there are times when he does not wear too well. Perhaps he was too much a man of his time, achieving singlehanded the revolution in music that Manet, Monet, and Renoir did in painting, and Baudelaire, Mallarmé, and Rimbaud led in poetry. Yet on the whole, his place remains eminent; music since his time is something other than it would be had he not lived; and his sensitive forms, his points of color, light, and shade, his rarefied melodies, his subtle intensities and tasteful emphases, opened many a magic casement.

TEN

STRAVINSKY

Although Igor Stravinsky is not a controversial figure, in the common understanding of the term, authoritative judgments still differ sharply as to his place in the musical firmament, and particularly as to which qualities it rests on, and in which works. At any rate, however, virtually all, including the public, agree that among the composers of the forty-five year period beginning in 1909, none has been more important, influential, original, and interesting than he. Hence his music has been selected in this study as probably the most representative example of what is now called modern, contemporary, or living, music.

Paradoxically, only a very small part of his large production lies in the category of absolute music. In the list of his works, we find numerous ballet scores, operas, vocal settings with orchestra, concerti, and the like. There are but two symphonies (except for a very early insignificant work). There is some chamber music, but as such, it cannot serve as material for this survey, especially as it includes no work for both strings and winds. The problem of selecting suitable works to illustrate his use of accents is made still more difficult by the fact that his creative life comprises two distinct periods which, especially the latter, are further divided into practically as many sub-periods as the number of his works! Generally speaking, in the first main period, consisting of the great ballets *Firebird, Petrouchka,* and *Rite of Spring,* he "remained on the ground"; he composed scores which, with all their piquancy, elaborateness, originality, and audacity, were still in close enough correspondence with the cultural capacity of their day to win respected and delighted acceptance after at most a few hearings. Thereafter, in his second period (so far), he dedicated himself to brilliant and ingenious exercises in the use of musical resources, which have added enormously to the range of musical art, but the aesthetic value of which is still problematical, in the judgment of both the public and many of the most esoteric professionals. This second period has been variously called neo-classic, or abstract. Stravinsky's musical career thus presents a striking (and often remarked) parallel to that of the painter Picasso (with whom Stravinsky sometimes actually collaborated), who at approximately the same times had his relatively derivative period, and then his long, independent period of abstraction. They both began with making art out of life, and went on to making art out of other art, or out of their own theoretical lucubrations.

From Stravinsky's first period, *Petrouchka* will serve as well as any other work as an example of his use of accents. The first movement accompanies a carnival scene, full of people in colorful garb bustling about gaily and impulsively. While at certain points the music takes shape in specific dance-forms, most of it aims to project the general mood of a carnival in Russia, and could largely be interpreted as a Russian version of French impressionism. At its very beginning, this work opens up a new realm of tone. *(Fig. 91)* Two horns sound a slow trill, an open fifth alternating with a minor third; two clarinets do the same at double speed an octave higher; and above all these, one flute *

* All references are to the original version of the score, not the 1947 revision apparently made mainly in order to extend the copyright.

announces a melodic line, which intentionally has no more distinction than enough to identify the whole passage on its several reappearances. The tempo is a fast 3/4; the horns and clarinets are *mp,* the flute, *f.* The section of the opening material led by the flute is a five-bar phrase; in the first, second and fifth bars the flute does nothing but play a rising fourth, A to D, six times. In the first and fifth of those six instances, both the A and D are eighth-notes, slurred together; in all the others they are detached, the A being a sixteenth and the D, a dotted eighth tied to the same tone on the next beat, and in all these latter cases, both notes are always marked >.

This section's melodic invention is deliberately suppressed in order to highlight its rippling sheen. Yet the leading voice, being made up so largely of repetitions of the same dry interval, needs to be made viable; and it is for this purpose that the variations in the rhythm of that interval, and the accents, are there. The composer wishes the "Scotch" rhythm of the sixteenth and dotted eighth to be clearly distinguished from the smooth-flowing and connected pairs of equal eighth-notes, by making the most of the difference of rhythm and articulation. Therefore the factors called for in the accents are acuteness and color; volume would distort the linear flow of the theme, and while duration is not involved because it is already there, the A's should be made quite *staccato* in the interest of heightening character. So the accents of the A's are the rare type 15, those of the D's, type 13. At Number 14 in the score this theme enters as a counterpoint to a homely dance tune, but, significantly enough, this time all the intervals of a fourth are slurred and not accented. The purpose of the alteration evidently is to keep this theme from having so much character that it might take interest away from the dance tune.

At Number 3, the basses, celli, and bassoons enter with an embryonic version of a folksong-like theme which, a few pages later, becomes much extended, and in the full orchestra. Here the time signature is still 3/4, as at the opening, but the natural rhythm of this theme is decidedly duple, and is barred so at its full appearance. There are two ways of scoring a theme whose rhythm lies in a time signature other than the prevailing one. One is by prefixing its proper time signature to the staves of the instruments that carry it, thus burdening the conductor with the extra responsibility of keeping different time signatures coordinated. The other is to leave the time signatures unchanged but to cross-accent the odd theme to make its beats sound as they would if written in the time signature proper to them. In this instance the composer selected the latter method; and no other purpose of the accents presents itself, the accents being quite regularly on the alternate quarter beats. Accordingly, the procedure being a purely rhythmical device, there is no occasion for any kind of special color on the accented tones; and the duration factor would throw the theme out of kilter. The remaining factors, those of acuteness and volume, result in an accent of type 10. *(Fig. 92)*

A cardinal feature of Stravinsky's style (or styles) is his preoccupation with rhythm. With him melody and harmony play important roles too, of course, but ordinarily of lesser consequence. We are entitled, nay required, to take this trait into consideration in analyzing his accents, and in any example to look for evidence of his rhythm laboratory. A composer's general predilection is a legitimate element of the context of any given detail of his work.

For example, take next the well-known (to conductors) passage beginning at Number 7, which, with certain variations, recurs five times in this movement. *(Fig. 93)* The time signatures of the bars, the first time, are 3/8, 4/8, 2/8, three bars of 5/8, 3/8, 4/8, and four of 5/8. It has often been gravely proclaimed that among Stravinsky's missions was the liberation of music from the "tyranny of the barline." If he had written his changing rhythm patterns within unchanging bars, there would be something to support this contention. However, it seems to at least one seeker after musical truth that passages such as this, in which the bar-lines and time signatures shift to conform to the changing rhythm patterns, far from challenging the tyranny of the bar-line, serve only to fortify it.

Be that as it may, the passage begins with a bellow on the deep instruments, three grace notes descending scalewise to B flat; third trombone, tuba and timpani hit the B flat with an eighth-note, marked *sf.* The only accent of the basses and celli lies on the first grace note. This entrance is obviously meant to be really loud and vigorous, with two wallops, one on the first grace note, the other on the B flat. The basses and celli must throw their bows onto the string near the frog; theirs is the responsibility for the first wallop, but not the second, which will be amply furnished by the brass and timpani. The strings' accent is type 4, the others', type 18; the shortening factor is due to the acoustic need of getting out of the way, as well as the aesthetic intention to produce an abrupt effect.

So much for the first beat of this passage. On the second, the violins and violas enter *mf* on a second, D and E in two octaves; and they repeat it on every eighth-note in the passage save in the last four bars, and a few pairs which are tied over together. Every one not tied to its predecessor has a mark **Y** over it, similar to the C.P.E. Bach accent symbol. Simultaneously, the woodwinds have a *staccato* figure, *ff*, also in eighth-notes, the topmost voice of which, in two flutes in unison, has a > mark on the first note of the fourth and sixth bars, and no other accents. Both those bars are *crescendo* in both the strings and woodwinds; in the strings both succeeding bars, the fifth and seventh, are again "*mf* sub.", while the woodwinds are silent.

Firstly, we can be sure that the C.P.E. Bach symbols on the string parts are *not* accents; for when we look at the reprises of this passage, the symbols recur, on every note not slurred to its predecessor, as before, except that on a few notes we find, instead of such symbols, the symbol >. The latter, then, are the accented notes; the others can be best interpreted as if the whole passage had instead been marked "*sempre staccato e marcato.*" The woodwind accents can serve no purpose but (1) to mark the bar-lines with their irregular recurrences, which they can do but faintly at best, since they are on only two of many instruments; and (2) to provide a tiny twinkle twice along the line. The woodwind players have a hard job, since they enter *forte* and must make a *crescendo*. We must believe that at the end of the *crescendo* they are playing; if not *ffff*, at least *fff*. The accent of the topmost voice comes at the beginning of the *crescendo;* it should include the volume factor, to effectuate the two purposes for which it can exist; so in both the accented bars the flutes will be playing these dynamics: *ffff-ff* $<$ *fff* +. In addition, an acute attack will be called for, and since the notes are *staccato,* no duration factor is involved, but the color factor should be included for the twinkle. Hence the accent type should be 4.

The last four bars of the passage, all in 5/8 time, contain but two triads, a fourth apart, each one, except the first, occurring on two successive eighth-notes, then leaping to the other. *(Fig. 93)* So the first chord of every bar has to be a different one in the series, until the fifth bar, which would be like the first if it should ever come around, but it never does. In all the winds there is a > on the first note of every bar; in the strings there is just one note, on the beginning of every bar, the first one only being marked *sf.* The timpani and bassoons, also unaccented, celli and basses play nothing but the first note of the first bar.

The first-bar accent is obviously the strongest of all, (1) because of the larger number of instruments playing than on any of the succeeding ones, (2) because that is the only one on which the strings are accented at all, and (3) because a quick slurred triplet in the woodwinds, practically a rush of grace notes, leads into it. Because of reason (3), the woodwinds cannot have an acute attack, but they should have the volume factor. Color and lengthening are surely not called for—in some halls shortening may be necessary—so this accent should be of type 5 or 21. The remaining woodwind accents, and all those in the brass, can and should have the acute factor, making them type 2 or 12, as should also the one in the strings.

This whole passage well epitomizes the merry confusion of a carnival, with its harmonies in a state of irresolution, no melody at all, and its rhythms strong and dislocated. It abruptly yields to a brief but more fully orchestrated return of the opening material, then a brief appearance of hand-organ music, when it returns, abruptly also, this time without any accents except on the first note, as before, and on one note in the flutes. The figure of the final 5/8 bars contains not two triads but three, all a fourth apart, and there are five bars of them; also at one point one triad gets a triple instead of merely a double repetition. Thus does Stravinsky constantly vary and emphasize his rhythmic material.

The third and fourth times the passage appears, all the tied over notes in the violins and violas are accented, as well as one at the beginning of one bar which is not tied over. Even though a pair of tied eighth-notes on the same pitch equal one quarter-note, there seems no reason for having the accent affect the duration of the second eighth note either way. The accents should clearly have the acute factor, and volume, sustained for one-eighth's value. There appears no occasion for the application of color of any kind. Hence the type of accent for all the accented notes here is 10.

At the last appearance of the 5/8 triad figure, at Number 26, the first note of the strings is marked *sff sempre*—and there are three more bars with a note on the first beat of each. This is the only example we have encountered of an accent applying to a note not individually marked with any kind of accent symbol. This device, using the word *sempre,* is seldom used, but it is as valid a means of indicating accents as any. Now there are eight bars of the figure, the second four bars bringing back the figure with three triads and introducing a new trombone counterpoint. *(Fig. 94)* The latter consists of six eighth-notes, twice, each time beginning and ending on the beginning of a bar, with an accent on each note, and *forte.* This figure surely needs acute attacks on every note, also a volume factor (the rest of the orchestra being *ff*), and a good brassy ring. A lengthening factor would help this figure to cut through, but how can one apply it when the instrument chosen is the trombone? Yet an attempt can be made, and with some chance of success, as all the notes are attainable in the first three positions, thus reducing the slide shifting to a minimum. So let us choose type 17 for these accents, the lengthening factor being to the extent to which the players can manage.

Comments on the remainder of the first movement can add little to our survey. Doubtless it has begun to look as if the great majority of Stravinsky's accents are percussive rather than expressive—and such an impression would indeed be very near the truth. Nonetheless, let us call attention to one of the minority, at Number 54 in the score, where the English horn, *mp,* plays a melody through a small section of the orchestra, which is *piano (Fig. 95).* The music parallels Petrouchka's sorrowful desire for both freedom and the ballerina, and is of appropriately yearning and lugubrious character. In a moderate four, the melody consists of two repeated notes, on each of the first two beats, *porta-mento,* and a third, on the last two beats, one degree of the scale above. This third note is preceded by a grace note, on the degree below it, and it has an accent. It surely should be extended to its full value, with expressive color, though without the volume factor; nor can it have an acute attack because of the combination of character and dynamics, and also the grace note; hence its type is 23, a genuinely expressive and lyrical accent.

At the very end of the second movement an odd marking appears: *più sf,* after a chord marked *sf,* both *pizzicato* in the strings, the last dynamic mark being *fff.* This can be explained by the fact that Stravinsky is a practical man of the theater, and as such, couched his directions in a "musical vernacular" which would probably be more foolproof than a logically correct equivalent. Thus we can understand this direction as a telescoping of *più f, sf.*

The last movement returns to the carnival, but with new music. When the general merrymaking is at its height, it is suddenly cut short at Number 125 by the appearance of Petrouchka fleeing from, and then felled by, the Moor. The interruption is represented in the orchestra by a sustained high note, *crescendo,* in the muted trumpets, one of which continues *fff* with a thematic fragment consisting of three descending sixteenth notes, then a higher quarter note, all accented. *(Fig. 96)* The moment is a tense, grim one, and the stabbing sound of the trumpet should be so considered. There being just one instrument involved, already marked *fff,* the volume factor can hardly be intended; but color is certainly conceived, as is the acute factor. As to duration, the three sixteenths should be "punched," that is, shortened—while the quarter, to bring out its starkness, should be lengthened. Accordingly, the accents of the sixteenths are type 15, while that of the quarter is type 14. The accents in the English horn in the next bar are similar in interpretation to those on the trumpet's sixteenth-notes, and should be the same type.

The death of Petrouchka is an apt point at which to close our study of the accents of Stravinsky's first period. Petrouchka is a sympathetic figure, puppet though he be—and the composer has surrounded him with superb music that would not be unworthy of a human character, and which lends itself readily to enjoyment and comprehension in the light of a healthy acquaintance of music in general. Perhaps in the deaths of both Petrouchka and the Sacrificial Virgin in the *Rite of Spring,* Stravinsky's link with the past also snapped. Then he was purged and free to sally forth on untried adventures and blaze new trails.

The music of Stravinsky's second period is as remote and forbidding as that of his first is accessible and colorful. At the end of a long and illustrious life, the romantic movement had shuddered to a convulsive death with Mahler, Reger, the pre-dodecaphonic Schönberg, and the rest. No doubt it was high time for it to give way to something else, something new, as it had been a century before. And to many the spare, sinewy, transparent texture that Stravinsky developed was a refreshing, cleansing change from the flabby and bloated structures in which the romantic movement had finally disintegrated. But whether the glassy stare that he turned to the world after 1914 is to set the style of the next prevailing school of music is a question which is still a long way from being answered in the affirmative. Here we find dissonances forced into harness together with ruthless logic (or often, apparently, lack of logic), and great importance given to the play of rhythmic devices. Percussion encroaches on the melodic instruments like cancer. Violence, the surprise attack, the repeated battering, become ordinary features of the composer's vocabulary. He is unable even to begin the slow movement of his *Capriccio* (1929-1949), in its quiet and stately pseudo-Bachian cantilena, without an accent, three accents occurring in the first two bars. He needs to punctuate with abrupt accented chords the introduction to a devotional work, the *Symphony of Psalms* (1930-1948). And in the entire exposition of the *Symphony in Three Movements* (1945), occupying 25 pages, it is scarcely an exaggeration to say that it is hard to find a single unaccented note, loud or soft, in any voice. That these accents are percussive rather than expressive is only too obvious from the complete context in all cases, and they are typical of Stravinsky's second period. Again, in that Symphony, as in Petrouchka, but much oftener, we find *ff sempre* and *sim.* after a bar of accented syncopations.

Shafts of knowledge have recently penetrated into areas formerly unknown, regions terrifying in their lifeless power or vastness—those of the atom, and of interstellar space. And consciousness of the new knowledge in both fields has become an established part of present-day life and thought. This music, so remote and astral, suggests the macabre and stupendous properties of both, and could be the musical counterpart of their share in today's living. It is made of the conventional tones; but in Stravinsky's hands, those tones are strained and mechanized to the point where they seem closely related to the planets floating in their inexorable orbits around the heavens, or the fantastic equations that outline the conditions on which matter becomes energy and vice versa—realities, yes, but the bare cerebral framework of reality: its scaffolding, if you will. This music can no more be stretched or compressed than can the paths of the planets, or any of the atomic equations; it is rigid, glazed, utterly soulless. To some it is also equally inevitable and cosmic.

With the advent of this attitude in music, we find that expressive types of accents have all but disappeared from the scene. No longer does music of this school compass the gentle, the warm, the intimate, the longing, the surging, the lingering on the instant of transfiguring beauty. It is brusque, impassive, and immovable. Diamonds cannot cut it. It does not court favor or attempt to charm or persuade; it stands aloof, indifferent, and impervious, remarkable and rather monstrous in its icy citadel.

It must also be noted that while Stravinsky's command of orchestration is supreme, he seems unable to completely emancipate himself from the rule of the piano. The scores of many of his orchestral works, including even the *Symphony in Three Movements,* contain indispensable parts for a piano, and in some works, for two pianos. The piano parts wield a percussive touch over the whole texture; and even when silent or absent, their percussive influence pervades the other instruments. In short, in Stravinsky's later orchestral style the leading edges of the tones are almost as all-essential as they are in piano literature. While he still needs the orchestra for conveying his many-voiced complexities, he largely abdicates his youthful lavish orchestral virtuosity in favor of a texture strictly limited, comparatively monochrome in color, and distinctly pianistic in contour.

No more need be said about the exposition of the first movement of the *Symphony in Three Movements.* Yet even in the development section, from Numbers 34 to 42, it seems almost impossible for Stravinsky to write an unaccented entrance on a sustained tone in the strings or wind. But he does not do this thoughtlessly. He does not do anything thoughtlessly. For instance, he calculates his dynamic balances to a nicety. At Number 40, in a 2/4 meter, flute, oboes, and clarinets enter

on the second quarter, *mp. (Fig. 97)* In the next bar the oboes drop out,

and the flute plays an octave lower than before—but marked *mf,* for no other reason than to be heard at strength equal to that of the higher octave; the clarinets continue in the same register as before, and to make sure that the dynamic increase of the flute will not be erroneously

shared by them, the composer marks their staff (*mp*). The only other instruments playing here are the horns and piano, and they maintain a steady *mp.* As for the analysis of the accents, they do not include the volume factor; for if they did, the flute would be *forte* at least momentarily in the second bar, and there is no reason why it should be. While an acute factor is certainly meant, the color factor is questionable. One could reason, in favor of it, that the woodwinds are specially selected for their timbre and idiom; and against it, that their sole use here is to sustain simultaneously all the tones sounded by the piano successively, thus becoming a collective aeolian damper pedal. So, depending on the undecided color factor, and its duration if included, the accent type should be 1, 3, or 13.

Let us examine one more accent before going on to some general comments. In the bar before Number 142 in the same Symphony, there

is a chord marked *p* following some chords marked *mf. (Fig. 98)* A sudden drop in volume is thus indicated, with no reduction in orchestration—on the contrary, the basses are added. On many of the accents in this Symphony, a volume factor is unquestionably called for; but on this accent, marked with the same symbol as the others, a volume factor would thwart the sudden drop in volume, and hence must be excluded.

Stravinsky utilizes a large variety of symbols to indicate the type and

quantity of his accents. In the Symphony and the *Capriccio,* these are
some of the markings encountered: > together with all dynamic marks,

$$> \qquad\qquad\qquad\qquad\qquad\qquad\qquad\qquad >$$

sfz, sfp, poco sfp, poco sfp sim., sf, sf e marcato, sfff, poco sf, ten.,

$$\qquad\qquad\qquad\qquad\qquad > \quad > \quad > \qquad\quad >$$

sempre poco sf e staccatissimo, poco, sfp, sf, poco sf, sempre sf stac-

$$\qquad\qquad\quad > \quad >$$

catissimo possibile, sempre sfp, sf in p. As in *Petrouchka,* he strives
admirably to make his intentions foolproof in practice, even if at
the cost of their logical correctness. If there were no system of accentuation confirmed through generations of music-making, all these
explanatory symbols would be very helpful; but since there is such a
system, all but two are quite superfluous.

The two exceptions are *sfp*—the tersest way indicating either one of
two nuances, which we have already met elsewhere—and *sf e marcato;*
the latter, however, solely because it is used in a context in which the
voice so marked is differentiated from others simultaneously marked
sf (étouffé) and *sf in p.* It is in such passages (Number 182 in the
Symphony) that one can perceive how enormously important *(Fig. 99)*
accents are to Stravinsky—they have actually grown into basic raw
materials of his art. We are familiar with counterpoint of voices, of
melodies, of rhythms, of timbres, and choirs—but here, for the first
time in musical history, we meet a counterpoint of accents!

Lest it be thought that this verdict was arrived at on insufficient evidence, let us see what Stravinsky himself has written:

I experience a sort of terror when, at the moment of setting to work and finding
myself before the infinitude of possibilities that present themselves, I have the feeling that everything is permissible to me. If everything is permissible to me, the best
and the worst; if nothing offers me any resistance, then any effort is inconceivable,
and I cannot use anything as a basis, and consequently every undertaking becomes
futile.

Will I then have to lose myself in the abyss of freedom? To what shall I cling
in order to escape the dizziness that seizes me before the virtuality of this infinitude? However, I shall not succumb. I shall overcome my terror and shall be re-
assured that I have the seven notes of the scale and its chromatic intervals at my
disposal, that strong and weak accents are within my reach, and that in all of these
I possess solid and concrete elements which offer me a field of experience just as vast
as the upsetting and dizzy infinitude that had just frightened me. It is into this field

that I shall sink my roots, fully convinced that combinations which have at their disposal twelve sounds in each octave and all possible rhythmic varieties promise me riches that all the activity of human genius will never exhaust. (*Poetics of Music,* 1947, p. 63f.)

Thus, in his own words, he proclaims that he considers accents, *per se,* to be among the fundamental resources of music. True, while there can be notes without accents, there cannot be an accent without a note; but aside from that disability, an accent, in Stravinsky's aesthetic, is a fully co-equal member of the family of tonal materials. He has severed the last link which had kept accents dependent, if ever so tenuously, on the musical context; in his storehouse, accents float, free, as readily available for use at any point as at any other, according to the composer's pleasure and/or purpose. And since, in his conception, accents are independent entities, not influenced by the context, and not analyzable therefrom, the specific quality of each one must be notated with thorough precision. This circumstance accounts for the great diversity of his symbols. That he thus aims to reduce the performer's role to the very minimum —little more than that of a skilled mechanic—is shown by further extracts from his writings:

No matter how scrupulously a piece of music may be notated, no matter how carefully it may be insured against every possible ambiguity through the indications of *tempo,* shading, phrasing, accentuation, and so on, it always contains hidden elements that defy definition, because verbal dialectic is powerless to define musical dialectic in its totality. The realization of these elements is thus a matter of experience and intuition, in a word, of the talent of the person who is called upon to present the music. . . .

How many times have I been the victim of these misdirected attentions from abstractors of quintessences who waste time splitting hairs over a *pianissimo,* without so much as noticing egregious blunders of rendition! Exceptions, you may say. Bad interpreters should not make us forget the good ones. I agree—noting, however, that the bad ones are in the majority and that the virtuosos who serve music faithfully and loyally are much rarer than those who, in order to get settled in the comfortable berth of a career, make music serve them. . . .

It was romantic music that unduly inflated the personality of the *Kapellmeister* even to the point of conferring upon him—along with the prestige that he today enjoys on his podium, which in itself concentrates attention upon him—the discretionary power that he exerts over the music committed to his care. Perched on his sibylline tripod, he imposes his own movements, his own particular shadings upon the compositions he conducts, and he even reaches the point of talking with a naive impudence of his specialties, of *his* fifth, of *his* seventh, the way a chef boasts of a dish of his own concoction. Hearing him speak, one thinks of the billboards that recommend eating places to automobilists: "At so-and-so's restaurant, his wines, his special dishes." (ibid. p. 123ff.)

These statements invite some further relevant comments:

1. All musicians of integrity should utter a lusty cheer for this authoritative condemnation of that bane of musical art, the prima donna conductor.

2. Obviously Stravinsky has had painful experiences with interpreters of his music.

But what composer has not? As he himself implies, he is certainly far from the first. Let us for a moment consider the problems of orchestral interpretation from the standpoint of not merits but faults. There are three principal categories of faults:

(a) those which demonstrably violate some physically measurable mark in the score (*e.g.,* wrong notes, wrong tempo, wrong rhythm, poor ensemble, wrong phrasing, wrong dynamics, bad intonation, rough tone, etc.)

(b) those which through ignorance, or erroneous judgment or analysis, misinterpret some mark in the score (*e.g.,* ornaments, accents); and

(c) those which, without violating or misinterpreting a single actual mark in the score, yet produce a result at variance with the composer's conception (*e.g.,* in matters of balance, tone quality, nuance, proportions, poetic content, and over-all "spirit"). It is this third category of faults that comprises the "hidden elements" to which Stravinsky refers, those matters for which writable symbols do not exist. He concedes that he, like all other composers, cannot insure his works against distortions in this category; as to them he is frankly at the mercy of the talent (and, he might have added, personal taste) of the interpreter.

The first two categories, however, involve elements which are not hidden at all. How does Stravinsky consider himself to have fared in making his works foolproof with regard to these? He claims to have successfully insured his works against distortions of the first category. In this, like all other composers, he is quite correct. Anybody with a score and a practiced ear (and better yet, a metronome) can readily identify, and prove, faults in this category.

As to faults of the second category, he says nothing specific, but he seems to believe that he has satisfactorily protected his music in that area also. Does he not say, "insured against every possible ambiguity through the indications of tempo, shading, phrasing, accentuation, and so on"? Hence does he not fully believe that he has marked his accents with the same infallibility as the tempi, shadings, and phrasings? And that their proper interpretation requires on the performer's part keen observation and an absence of both thought and learning?

That he is mistaken in that belief is demonstrated by the instances in his *Symphony in Three Movements* which have been pointed out, and many others in his later works which have not been individually pointed out, in which thought and learning on the performer's part are quite indispensable. Furthermore, his use of the symbol *sfp* utterly fails to clarify the ambiguity in which he and all other composers leave it, requiring just as much reasoning for its interpretation as it does in scores by other composers. Moreover, what are we to make of his

$>$

poco sf? On its face this symbol calls for a slight double accent. But how, if at all, is this to be differentiated from a full-size single accent? Most probably an answer exists; but its attainment is possible only through much thought and knowledge. Whatever it may be, it does *not* involve a larger accent being indicated by the symbol *sf* than by the symbol $>$; for one frequently finds such indications as "*sf leggiero.*"

3. Hence it is clear that his valiant attempt to prescribe in detail the exact form and size of every accent, without reference to both a body of knowledge and a method of analysis, has not succeeded. It, or some other system, may do so some day, and then the extant system of accentuation will be deservedly relegated to limbo. But he has not as yet brought this about—even for his own music.

ELEVEN

THE MUSIC OF AMERICA

Many as are the elements that all art music has in common internationally, the art music of every country that has produced any has its own distinct national character. This character, or group of characteristics, is more obvious in some composers' work than in others'; but once defined, it can be detected in greater or less degree in the bulk of the musical production of any given nation.

America has produced a respectable quantity of music throughout most of its history. Its composers have been dedicated men and women; and many of them have been highly gifted, others have been well schooled, and a few have been both. Yet until fairly recently, much of its most authentic music has issued from composers of very limited scope and craftsmanship; and its music that has not been so handicapped has been either too derivative in style and content, or too small in quantity, or insufficiently favored by the hazards and politics of the musical profession, to have been accepted as an influential voice rooted in American soil.

This survey will not undertake the irrelevant and delicate task of tracing the definitions, origins, and growth of the peculiarly American elements in music. Suffice it to say that general acclamation, fully shared by this writer, places George Gershwin and Aaron Copland prominently among the many composers who have written music that is both of high quality and unmistakably American.

Gershwin made his first steps toward fame and fortune in the field of commercial music. His own contributions, though, were marked by a persona' idiom so attractive and distinctive that he soon became one of the moguls of his trade. Accepting encouragement to do bigger and better things, he essayed works in larger and more serious forms, many of which may well remain loved for a long time; for they *are* New York, and Los Angeles, and Chicago, and Miami—though probably not Boston—the slick, jumpy, breezy, impudent, sophisticated, mundane, happy-go-lucky, sentimental, naughty, insecure, ribald, frenetic, gregarious creature with a heart of gold that America largely is. A show-business America, perhaps—but that is big business precisely because so much of America, and every typical American, loves it, needs it, is it.

To the untimely end of his life he remained unfinished in his craftsmanship and awkward in the handling of extended forms; nor did he ever lose touch with his Tin Pan Alley debut. His scores have been revised by some of his associates; and consequently several of them are available in two or more versions.

His most important work for orchestra without soloist is the tone poem *An American in Paris.* This is one of the works of which there are differing editions; and the task of arriving at definitive data is further confused by the curious fact that the printed orchestral parts do not entirely agree with any one score, and the still more curious fact that those parts are not even entirely in accord with one another. However, for the purpose of examining accents, some choice must be made, so we shall select the score in commonest use, the one revised by Campbell-Watson.

The first accent illustrative of Gershwin's special style is found early in the score, in the fifth bar after Number 2. *(Fig. 100)* In a lively 2/4, the solo trumpet, *forte,* introduces a motive consisting of four repeated sixteenth-notes, and an eighth-note one tone higher, all *staccato.* It then returns to the first note, which is accented and tied into the next bar. This accent creates a syncopation, a jazzy "kick" on the last after beat, but in this voice only. Hence it needs an acute factor, as well as volume. Color, too, of a jazzy nature, is called for, but as the duration factor is not involved, the type is 4. The reasons why it is not type 10 are, that the substance of the accent lies in the impact, there is a *diminuendo* on the end of the bar, and another voice immediately takes the lead in the next bar. That voice is the solo trombone, answering the figure, without being tied over into the bar following. The trombone should extend its last note to the full value, but without any accent factors remaining in the tone. For the first trumpet the type is thus a class C accent of types 4 plus 28.

A fuller illustration of Gershwin's pulse-dislocating trait comes at Number 3. *(Fig. 101)* The strings take up the trumpet motive in sequence, and since the motive spans but three eighths, it lies on a different beat of the bar each time. On each of the strings' eighth-notes, the winds, *forte,* and the cymbals, *mf,* join in, *staccato* and accented; and the cymbals are marked "stop quickly." Surely the cymbals, and most probably the winds also, are scored here for their characteristic sound; therefore the color factor should be in the accent, and so should the acute factor, to bring out the syncopation. The direction "stop quickly" in the cymbal part calls for a shortening of the tone, and since the winds share the cymbals' entrances, the shortening should also apply to them. The inclusion of the volume factor is very doubtful; for if it were present, the accented chords would tend to overbalance, particularly in the fifth member of the sequence where the motive lies in only the celli, basses, bassoons and bass clarinet. Therefore the accent should be of the rare type 3.

At Number 8 the horns, *forte,* go along in chromatically rising and descending triads, two to a bar, all marked $\overset{>}{sfz}.$ *(Fig. 102)* The bassoons share this voice; their last dynamic mark was *p,* and obviously here it should be *f,* but owing to Gershwin's lack of exactness in editing his scores, it is not. However, the dynamics question with bassoons is not vital, as they are scarcely audible anyway unless exposed. This voice lends insouciance to this passage, the principal part of which has no tonal relation whatever to it. It should be heard, then, subordinate in prominence only to the ascending main voice; and the double accents are nicely calculated to accomplish exactly that, with the type being 17. Technically speaking, of course, the lengthening factor cannot be applied in double quantity, as it is ordinarily consumed to its full extent by its first application.

From the seventh to the eighth bar after Number 8, the bass clarinet, *forte,* solo, makes an amusing downward leap of an augmented octave, and holds the last note for several bars. That last note is marked *sf-p* (praise be to Gershwin—the marking being his own—for avoiding the ambiguous *sfp*) which calls for an accent, still in *forte,* sustained for some space of time, then a termination of the accent features, whatever they may be, and a quick drop in the dynamic level to *piano. (Fig. 102)*

Now let us consider the elements of the accent itself. The note is a surprising one, and the surprise should be enhanced by an acute attack, and also a volume factor. As the bass clarinet is an instrument of distinctive timbre, the color should also be included; and as the duration factor of the complete tone is not involved, the accent type is 16. However, the line in the marking calls for some extension of the color factor—a matter of taste, somewhere from a quarter's value to a bar's. And a comic gasp can be added to the moment by a slight *rubato* on the accented note and its predecessor.

One of the main themes enters, *ff,* in the clarinets at Number 13: an eighth-note, repeated in four sixteenths, another eighth a third higher, then a skip down of an augmented fourth on the beginning of the second bar (still 2/4), and sustained throughout the bar. There are accents on the first of these notes (which this time is preceded by a run of three grace notes) and the last. The matter that concerns us here is not these accents, but the omission of an accent; for in every later appearance of the theme, the penultimate note also is accented, and it ought to be here too. *(Fig. 103)* For some reason Gershwin himself insisted on the omission of the accent here. What happens by leaving it unaccented is that the clarinets fail to give it the bright jocularity, as well as its full time-value, that it amply deserves, thus dropping onto the next note a mite too soon, and as a result tearing the heart out of the theme. The deficiency is serious, and should be rectified at rehearsals.

A gently expressive accent is encountered in the English horn part at Number 40—calling for a little "leaning on" the note. The theme is one previously introduced in quite a brash character, and here it takes on a reflective tinge. *(Fig. 104)* This accent ought to be a plain one, with a pronounced color factor, of both timbre and expressiveness, and without the volume factor—type 22. In the third bar after Number 40, this motive, which spans two bars, is repeated with its melody ornamented by neighboring tones; and throughout the repetition there is no accent at all. Thus, if the accent were a strong one, the repetition would be anticlimactic.

This theme undergoes yet another transformation at Number 43, where it is heard *pp* in augmentation, and in a series of six parallel polytonal chords. *(Fig. 105)* In the woodwinds the first five are slurred, but in the strings all six are *pizzicato*. And in the woodwinds only, the sixth chord is marked $\overset{>}{sfz\text{-}pp}$. This, also, is a double accent. The fact that the strings are *pizzicato* does not necessarily call for an acute attack; and an acute attack here would disturb the tranquil mood of the passage. In fact, the woodwind players should not breathe before the accent, but continue blowing, and effectuate the accent without either an interruption in the stream of sound they are producing, or a marked inception of the accented note. The accent is surely one of color, and for it to have perceptible significance it should also have the volume factor. There is an additional reason for the volume factor, viz., that the hyphen before *pp* shows a return to *pp* after the accent rather than a *pp* condition of the accent, so the type is 25.

Two especially lovely accents follow this one: the first in the solo horn, closed, in the bar before 44 *(Fig. 106),* the other in the bass trombone, solo, in the second bar after 45. They are both on the note which was not accented, but should have been, in the motive introduced in the clarinets at Number 13. The passage surrounding the present point is a dreamy transition to a "blues" mood in sharp contrast to the jaunty one prevalent hitherto. Fragments of the preceding themes are heard meditatively recollected in tranquillity. At the first of these two accents the clarinet theme, instead of skipping down an augmented fourth, rises a semitone, to a tone of a polytonal chord, the entrance of which can be quite enchanting. Surely the accented note before it ought to heighten the expectancy, and make the magic of this instant as sure as possible; and that can be achieved with a sensitive nuance consisting of expressive color, a lengthening factor, and—a tiny pause thereafter. Anything else could shatter this fragile moment.

A few bars later the trombone has still another variant of the same motive, and its accent should be the same as the horn's, which is type 23; a hesitation after the accented note will likewise add to it a breath of wonder. This discussion should be a sufficient guide to all the accents in the remainder of the work.

Gershwin's music lacks much in technical mastery and high seriousness, but it largely makes up for these shortcomings with flights of incandescent imagination, and with its warm and appealing utterance of the voice of the common man. That the conventional system of accentuation is as well fitted to such music as to that of the Olympian masters, assisting its communicative content, attests to its flexibility and general usefulness.

Aaron Copland's background was the same as Gershwin's—a Jewish immigrant family in New York. And also like Gershwin, his earliest creative influences were associated with jazz, but in a different way: technically well schooled, he never composed for the multitude, but he did inject a good deal of jazz into his concert and theater works. In his maturity he put away such youthful pastimes and produced some works of serious consequence, scores for ballets of the American frontier. How this evolution took place from an origin similar to Gershwin's would make an interesting biographical study; for the purpose of this survey, suffice it to say that it did. Copland's later scores are lean and angular, well suited to the plains and pioneers they characterize.

One of his most representative and successful works is *Appalachian Spring,* supporting a ballet of pioneer farm life. The revised score, which we shall examine, is a condensation of all the music except those sections in which the interest is primarily choreographic. Many of the accents in it, including the first two, are of considerable interest. After a leisurely introduction, an *allegro* movement opens with one of the basic rhythms of the work, two eighth-notes and a quarter. This rhythm occupies the whole bar, on the chord of A major; and the last note, A, is tied over to a whole note with a *fermata,* in the next bar. The violins, violas, and piano play in unison, and the xylophone chimes in on the first and fourth beats, on which the accents fall in all parts, marked >. The dynamic level is *f,* and the strings and piano are marked *"vigoroso." (Fig. 107)*

Other than that and the accents, there is no mark which could indicate the intended length of any of the eighth-notes. But since this music is obviously connected with an animated dance, any rudimentary perception would require the eighth-notes to be certainly no broader than normal, and probably even somewhat shorter. The quarter-notes, though, should have at least normal duration. The reason for this is, that as this basic rhythm pervades the bulk of the work, it must be enunciated with the inflection that will give it the most salient and appropriate character; and that truly seems to call for a substantial pulse on the even-numbered beats, especially the fourth. Besides, the composer shows that he conceived it this way, at Number 15, where the solo flute has this motive; and it has a line over every quarter-note. Also, the direction *vigoroso,* or the equivalent, is ordinarily executed by a shortening of the shorter notes and a broadening of the longer ones.

Accordingly, the first accent should have the shortening factor, as well as the acute and volume factors, making it type 12. The second accented note, being tied to its successor, cannot have a duration factor except for the prolongation of the volume factor in the accent; but it does seem most plausible that the strings should sustain this (the percussion instruments, including the piano, being of course unable to). It is a good plan to have them keep moving their bows back and forth at individual rates, thus keeping the tone alive and strong. The accent type is thus 11. Since the next note is also accented, there is no chance of the next phrase being begun with less vigor than that with which the first one ended. The third and fourth bars are similar in principle to the first two. They are followed by two bars of *piano,* one bar of

silence, and two more of *piano*. *(Fig. 108)* The former of these last
two bars begins with a quarter rest, after which the violins and piano
strike a sustained A in octaves, marked $\overset{>}{sfp}$. One beat later, the woodwinds enter *mp*.

The usual ambiguity of the marking *sfp* is much less pronounced
in this case than in most (for a comment on that ambiguity, see
page 107.) Here the *p* in the marking indicates that the sustained tone
in the violins, after the accent, should be *piano,* to let the woodwinds
through; but even for this purpose it is unnecessary except as a pre-
caution, since the prevailing dynamic level is already *piano*.

The modern dance, as well as modern music, favors effects that
startle and are deliberately and entirely unanticipated; this entrance
is one such effect, coinciding with a sudden movement in the choreog-
raphy. But it is not a terrific crash, being played by only the violins and
the piano. Hence, the tightening net of logic pins this accent down
more and more as no exception to what our study would normally
show it to be: an accent in *piano,* and being a double accent, in double
quantity. The accent factors should unquestionably include acuteness
and volume. As there is no evident requirement of color, the type is 2.
The piano, whose note is a dotted half, should be struck smartly,
though not loudly, and the keys should be held down to the end of
the bar.

At Number 8, in *forte,* a rising figure of a quarter-note, two eighths
and two quarters enters *fugato*. In all entries the first quarter-note
is accented. *(Fig. 109)* It is a strong note in the phrase, and the two
eighths have the effect of transmitting its mass to the next quarters. But
to do this, the eighths have to take that mass directly from the note
that has it; *i.e.,* that note must pass it on to them, and so must stay
very much alive up to the next note. Thus, it must have the lengthening factor, as well as the acute and volume factors—the movement being
still quite vigorous—and the type is 11.

In passing, one can note, from Numbers 11 to 14, a conspicuous
illustration of two important and related tendencies in this work: to
exaggerate the weight of the last beat of the bar, and to feel the eighths
short and the quarters long.

A quite original bit of writing appears at Number 19, where the violins play a slow melody, *forte,* muted, marked *"molto espress.,"* every note of which is bowed and accented. *(Fig. 110)* Copland is quite capable of writing consonant harmonies; and the astringent quality of those in this passage indicates a mood quite at variance with a sense of security and well-being. This music bespeaks strain, urgency, and tension; every note is to be sustained, and with a highly charged character. The style of bowing, in string players' parlance, could be termed *détaché marcato.* The accents, therefore, must all have the acute, volume, color, and lengthening factors, adding up to type 17.

There can be no doubt that Copland knows well the sound he wants his music to make, certainly where the accents are concerned, and he strives to clarify, and not complicate, the interpreter's task. At Number 28, at the beginning of an angular passage for violins and violas alone, he writes in the score "heavy accents." Without articulately specifying which of the four factors he wants, he does show that he does want all of those that make for weight, whatever their nomenclature. In our table those are, of course, length, volume, and color, of a heavy quality; in addition, an acute factor would be appropriate, so the type again is 17. Since some of the accented notes are eighths, and between the beats, and not susceptible of interpretation to properly fit the composer's conception from the context alone, his written guide is needed, and his furnishing of it is highly welcome.

Double accents occur at many points in the score, notably between Numbers 35 and 41. These should need no comment beyond what has already been stated. The accents between Numbers 43 and 44 are probably of the rare type 9. *(Fig. 111)* The dynamics are *mezzo-forte,* later *forte,* and the score plainly shows that the limitation of the volume to these levels is deliberately desired. Further, the shortening factor is clearly called for, by the incisive character of the passage, and the *staccato* dots, which, once the character of the passage is properly diagnosed, are actually superfluous. The remaining accents in *Appalachian Spring* call for no further comment.

Thus the music of America—whether it be the gaudy expression of the cities, or the stark portrayal of the open spaces, or presumably, too, any other national attitudes that may find musical utterance—is no exception whatever to the literature served by the universally accepted principles of accentuation. No such exception has been encountered nor, if there be any, is the writer cognizant of it.

While we have pointed out numerous examples of symbols for a limited accent, such as *sfp,* or *poco sf,* the writer has never seen any example of a symbol for an augmented accent, other than those that have been pointed out: the double accents, the accents explained by words in the score, and the symbol ∧, the last of which is to be discussed in the Appendix. No symbol such as *molto* >, or *sfsf,* has been found in any work known to the writer; the *sff*'s and such that we have seen are nothing but abbreviations, longer than necessary, of "accent in a dynamic level of *forte* (or *fortissimo,* as the case may be)" —and they all do occur where the dynamic level actually is *forte* or *fortissimo* anyway.

Therefore we can confidently conclude that the principles of accent interpretation and performance set forth in this survey have in fact been those which the composers of orchestral music have invoked with their accent symbols. Of course the composers are "on the inside" of their music; to them the marks they inscribe on their score paper are merely the shorthand for the music they strive to convey. It is then the task of the performers to recreate in themselves the spirit of the music—to "get inside" it, as the composer had been, by dint of all the insight they can summon up, and all the sympathetic study they can lavish. The writer hopes that, where accents are concerned, he has furnished some assistance toward the latter process.

In conclusion, the writer would like to make some suggestions, which the reader can have anticipated. It is too much to ask, and quite unnecessary, that composers write, along with each accent, the number of the type they conceive. But there is no reason why accents intended to take effect after a tone's inception cannot readily be written accordingly, instead of directly above or below the accented note (see the discussion of Cannabich, and of Beethoven's violin concerto, for illustrations of this point). It would also be helpful to scrap all accent symbols save two—it does not matter which two—for a multiplicity of symbols only produces confusion, defeating the composers' very purposes. One of the two remaining symbols would stand for regular accents, which are integrally woven into the context, and the other, for the extraordinary, or absolute, accents, which are not. Together with any occasional explanatory words, they should provide for all the range of accentuation ever needed by any composer—if the performers are worthy of the name.

APPENDIX

As has been pointed out in the body of this survey, there are some accents of the romantic and post-romantic periods that lie outside the regular system, being the exaggerated or extraordinary accents symbolized by the mark $\wedge$ (or $\vee$).

One of the foundations of biology is the abundantly proved fact that the descendants of any pair of parents, animal or vegetable, exhibit the characteristics of the parents according to a definite scheme of distribution, also that species change only gradually and over a long series of generations. Yet once in a great while, a species puts forth an individual markedly different from any ancestor, whose characteristics are not explicable by the universal laws of descent. Such abrupt and conspicuous deviations in a species are termed sports, or mutations. And while they constitute violations of basic biological generalizations, they still take place within the jurisdiction of biology; and consequently that science must, and does, take cognizance of them.

In the same way, the ∧ accents can be considered "sports" of music. While they are deviations from generally prevalent truths, one cannot say that they do not exist, and therefore the study of music takes cognizance of them; but their properties are to be judged on their own erratic bases, only remotely related to normal forces.

As we have observed before, the romantic movement brought in its train many new resources of its vehement rhetoric—harmonic, melodic, coloristic, formal, stylistic, and rhythmical. Its fundamental difference from the classic style consists of the importance it gives to the part in relation to the whole, and to content in relation to form. In it, the tasty detail, the striking motive, the epigram, and whimsy, come into their own; and in orchestral music, it reached its full flowering first in the life and works of Robert Schumann.

No other composer pounces on a chord with such delight and excitement, as a kitten pounces on a ball. He is Youth itself, enraptured with the wonder of life, love, and beauty; and the value of his music rests largely on its fresh impetuosity. If one were to listen to it as to the music of one of the more Olympian masters, one would sense how unbecoming to a grown man these pouncings are. Yet the forthright fervor of his music is often so persuasive that it sweeps all along before it—in any event, up to the point where familiarity dulls the glow of spontaneity.

The role of an accent is that of a highlight of a progression extended (if only briefly) in time, significant only in relation to what is before and/or after it. But a ∧ accent breaks out of such a role. While it does not become, as in the later Stravinsky, a basic item of material in itself, it does become something in between: (1) a tone or chord, intended to be electrifying independently, by its harmony, volume, tone color or energy, all but regardless of its placement in the surrounding context; (2) a tone or chord whose emphatic force and prominence is meant to be limited by nothing but the maximum physical capacity of the instrument to produce it; or (3) an imposing, portentous proclamation, in a character more monumental than would be indicated by a regular accent, even a double one. These accents, as a rule (though there are a few exceptions), occur in a loud dynamic level.

Schumann's use of the ∧ accent can readily be observed throughout such works as the *Third Symphony,* and the *Cello Concerto.* Of course it does not appear in the slow and quiet movements; but where it does, it is used with about equal frequency in each of these categories; and which one it is, is ordinarily quite obvious, as well as academic, for the manner of playing them all is exactly the same—except that in the case of (2), the sheer volume might be somewhat ampler than in the case of the others. No example should be considered as (2) unless it cannot be otherwise classified.

Had Wagner written nothing but *"Die Meistersinger,"* his place as one of the few greatest composers of all time might be even more secure than it is. In recent times there has been a tendency in critical quarters to disparage the man because of the pomposities, longueurs, and deceptions in his other works—and also, to be entirely truthful, because of his powerful chromatic polyphony, from the influence of which it was well-nigh impossible for composers to extricate themselves for decades. The faults are largely his unsuccessful attempts to make music do more than what even he could make it do: to express the transcendental, the absolute, the unsearchable. The odd thing is that he came closest to succeeding in *"Die Meistersinger,"* the work that much less than any other shows the strains of striving for it. For better or worse, it is mostly by the imperfect, though more typical, works, those resplendent and delirious pageants, that he is known to the public; and naturally it is in them that the much larger ratio of ∧ accents occurs. Those accents are not so much embellishments of the lashing and heaven-storming style as inherent necessities of it; and most of them are in group (3). One finds them—to mention the irreducible minimum of examples—in the "faith" motive of *Parsifal (Fig. 112);* in the return of the opening theme of the *Tannhäuser* overture; in the apotheosized *Siegfried's* horn theme in the "funeral march"; at the climax of the *Lohengrin* prelude; in the chords of the "wanderer" theme as they bestride the whirlwind of the prelude to Act 3 of *Siegfried;* and even in the exquisite and leisurely Siegfried Idyll, in the section in which the two main themes are combined. In the *Tristan* prelude, too, just before the climax, where the horns and celli sing the opening motive—the last eighth-note of the motive carries a ∧ . The motive being *legato,* an acute attack is impossible, so the amplitude of the accent must be effectuated by liberal helpings of the other factors. The expressive importance of this note is thus obvious, except to many conductors, who would do well to bear it in mind more than they do at the beginning of the prelude, as well as right here. *(Fig. 113)*

Debussy, too, is among those who have written ∧ accents in most of their orchestral works. In *La Mer,* the first one appears at Number 10, on the accented note of the theme for celli alone, when the theme lies in the woodwinds. Again, at the end of the first movement, ∧ accents sit on the tremendous last three chords—the last being the eerie one whose mysterious "added sixth" evaporates over the horizon, leaving behind the bare triad, like a handful of seaweed. *(Fig. 114)* In the second movement, Debussy reserves the ∧ accent for the climactic chord, in the fifth bar after Number 28. And in the last movement it appears over the notes of the cyclical brass chorale theme as it returns for the last time, four bars before Number 61—a passage oddly reminiscent of the Rhine flooding the hall of the Gibichungs.

Were this survey to undertake to interpret every accent in only the most important works of the orchestral literature, it would have to be many times its present size, and might never come to an end. As it is, the writer has essayed to convey a sense of the importance and interest of accents, and hopes that he has selected a sufficiently various sampling of them to provide a method of analysis and interpretation, if only by analogy, of any accent likely to be encountered. If in so doing he has facilitated the approach of any music lovers to beauty, he will not have written this book in vain.

ILLUSTRATIONS

3

6 cont.

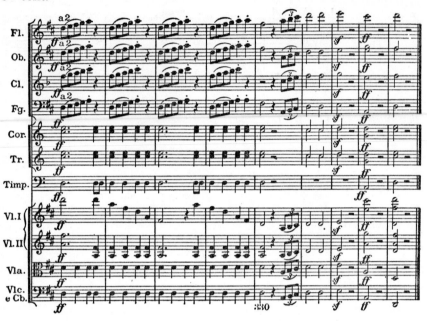

7

7 cont.

Adagio

2 Flauti

2 Obei

2 Clarinetti in B

2 Fagotti

2 Corni in Es

2 Trombe in Es

3 Tromboni

Timpani in Es-B

Violino I

Violino II

Viola

Violoncello e
Contrabasso

9

11

12   cont.

13

14

15

16

19

21

23   **24**

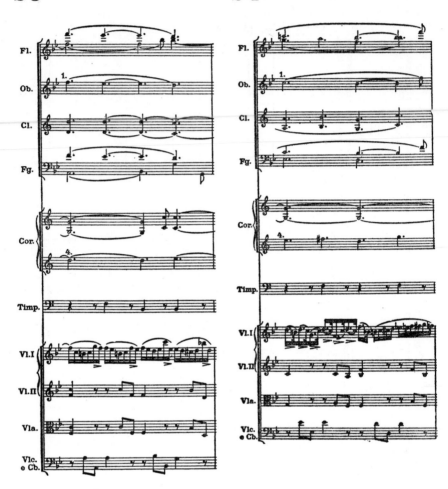

26

28

30

185

31

31 cont.

32 cont.

34

34 cont.

38

260

41

42 cont.

201

42 cont.

43 cont.

45

46   46 cont.

47

48 cont.

49 cont.

50 cont.

51

52

53

Allegro non troppo

55

57

58

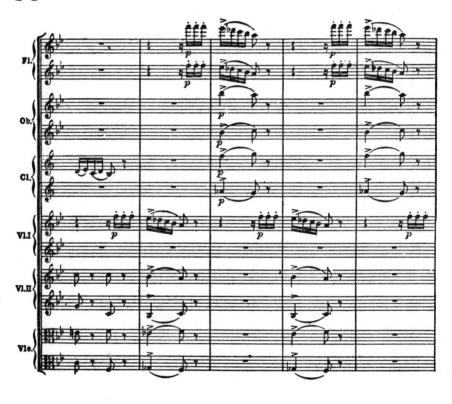

6 0

61   cont.

62

63

64

65

65 cont.

Tempo di trepak, molto vivace

Flauto I

Flauti II . III

Oboi I II

Corno Inglese

Clarinetto I in A

Clarinetto II in A

Clar. Basso in B

Fagotti I II

Corni in F
I
II
III
IV

Trombe in A

Tromboni Tenori

Tr. Basso e Tuba

Timpani G D

Tamburino

Violini I

Violini II

Viole

Celli

C-Bassi

67

69

70

71

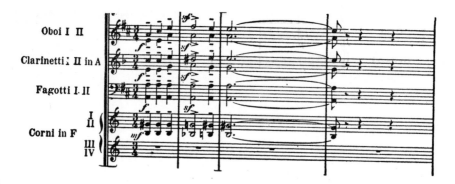

7 3

Adagio (♩=54)

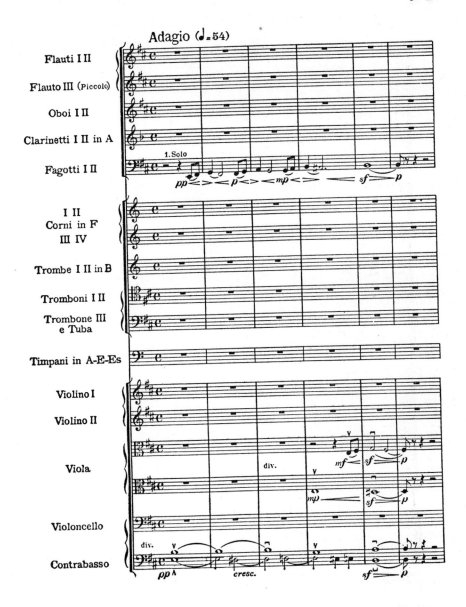

75

Allegro non troppo (♩ = 116)

78

79

Volles Zeitmaß. *(sehr lebhaft.)*

79 cont.

81

82

82 cont.

Permission for reprint granted by Jean Jobert, Paris, France, copyright owners; Elkan-Vogel Company, Philadelphia, Pa., agents.

83

Permission for reprint granted by Jean Jobert, Paris,
France, copyright owners; Elkan-Vogel Company,
Philadelphia, Pa., agents.

84

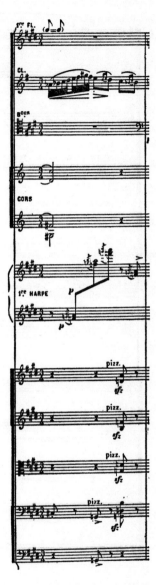

Permission for reprint granted by Jean Jobert, Paris, France, copyright owners; Elkan-Vogel Company, Philadelphia, Pa., agents.

85

Permission for reprint granted by Jean Jobert, Paris,
France, copyright owners; Elkan-Vogel Company,
Philadelphia, Pa., agents.

Permission for reprint granted by Durand et Cie.,
Paris, France, copyright owners; Elkan-Vogel Company, Philadelphia, Pa., agents.

86 cont.

Permission for reprint granted by Durand et Cie.,
Paris, France, copyright owners; Elkan-Vogel Company, Philadelphia, Pa., agents.

Permission for reprint granted by Durand et Cie.,
Paris, France, copyright owners; Elkan-Vogel Company, Philadelphia, Pa., agents.

88

Permission for reprint granted by Durand et Cie.,
Paris, France, copyright owners; Elkan-Vogel Company, Philadelphia, Pa., agents.

Permission for reprint granted by Durand et Cie.,
Paris, France, copyright owners; Elkan-Vogel Company, Philadelphia, Pa., agents.

89

Permission for reprint granted by Durand et Cie., Paris, France, copyright owners; Elkan-Vogel Company, Philadelphia, Pa., agents.

90

Permission for reprint granted by Durand et Cie., Paris, France, copyright owners; Elkan-Vogel Company, Philadelphia, Pa., agents.

90 cont.

Permission for reprint granted by Durand et Cie.,
Paris, France, copyright owners; Elkan-Vogel Company, Philadelphia, Pa., agents.

91

Copyright Edition Russe de Musique. Used by permission of Boosey & Hawkes.

92

Copyright Edition Russe de Musique. Used by permission of Boosey & Hawkes.

Copyright Edition Russe de Musique. Used by permission of Boosey & Hawkes.

93 cont.

Copyright Edition Russe de Musique. Used by permission of Boosey & Hawkes.

Copyright Edition Russe de Musique. Used by permission of Boosey & Hawkes.

94 cont.

Copyright Edition Russe de Musique. Used by permission of Boosey & Hawkes.

Copyright Edition Russe de Musique. Used by permission of Boosey & Hawkes.

97

98

99

Copyright 1946 by Associated Music Publishers,
Inc., used by permission.

100

Copyright 1929 by New World Music Corporation, reproduced by permission.

101

Copyright 1929 by New World Music Corporation,
reproduced by permission.

265

102   102 cont.

Copyright 1929 by New World Music Corporation,
reproduced by permission.

103

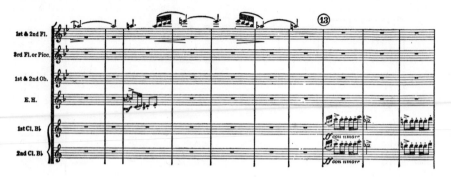

104

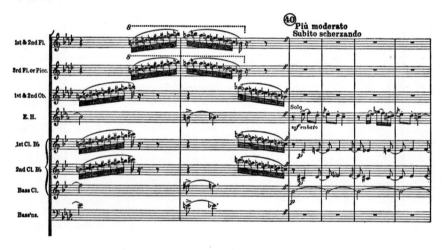

Copyright 1929 by New World Music Corporation,
reproduced by permission.

Copyright 1929 by New World Music Corporation,
reproduced by permission.

106

Copyright 1929 by New World Music Corporation, reproduced by permission.

Copyright 1945 by Hawkes & Son (London) Ltd.,
reproduced by permission.

108

Copyright 1945 by Hawkes & Son (London) Ltd.,
reproduced by permission.

Copyright 1945 by Hawkes & Son (London) Ltd.,
reproduced by permission.

110

Copyright 1945 by Hawkes & Son (London) Ltd., reproduced by permission.

111

Copyright 1945 by Hawkes & Son (London) Ltd.,
reproduced by permission.

112

113

114

Permission for reprint granted by Durand et Cie., Paris, France, copyright owners; Elkan-Vogel Company, Philadelphia, Pa., agents.